Rowland Evans Robinson

Uncle Lisha's Shop

Rowland Evans Robinson

Uncle Lisha's Shop

Life in a Corner of Yankeeland

Rowland Evans Robinson

Uncle Lisha's Shop

Life in a Corner of Yankeeland

ISBN/EAN: 9783743423107

Manufactured in Europe, USA, Canada, Australia, Japa

Cover: Foto ©ninafisch / pixelio.de

Manufactured and distributed by brebook publishing software (www.brebook.com)

UNCLE LISHA'S SHOP.

LIFE IN

A CORNER OF YANKEELAND.

BY

ROWLAND E. ROBINSON.

NEW YORK:
FOREST AND STREAM PUBLISHING CO.
1887.

By FOREST AND STREAM PUBLISHING CO.

THE DANVIS FOLK.

The boundaries of the township of Danvis are not more clearly defined than the limits of the county of Charlotte, in which it is situated. Suffice it to say that it is in the State of Vermont, backed at the east by the mountains that gave the State its name, and shut out from the valley of the Champlain by outlying spurs of the same range. Thus fortified against the march of improvement, its inhabitants longer retained the primitive manners, speech, and customs of the earliest settlers of Vermont than did the population of the lake towns, whose intercourse with the great centres of trade and culture was more direct and frequent.

It is all changed now : Danvis has daily mails, the telegraph almost touches its border, and its mountains echo the shrieks of locomotives and the roar of railroad-trains. The people, generally, wear as fine and modern clothes as any country folk, and it is doubtful whether there is one adult who has not seen something of the bustle and life of at least one of Vermont's two cities, if not those of even greater marts. An aristocracy has sprung up, and people are losing the neighborly kindness of the old times when none were rich and none were poor, and all were in greater measure dependent on each other. In fact, the Danvis folk are no better now than their lowland neighbors, who therefore no longer despise them.

CONTENTS.

CHAPTER	PAGE
I. THE SCHOOL MEETING IN DISTRICT 13,	7
II. UNCLE LISHA'S SPRING GUN,	17
III. IN UNCLE LISHA'S SHOP,	29
IV. CONCERNING OWLS,	34
V. UNCLE LISHA'S COURTING,	40
VI. HOW ZENE BURNHAM COME IT ON HIS FATHER,	48
VII. A RAINY DAY IN THE SHOP,	54
VIII. THE TURKEY SHOOT AT HAMNER'S,	64
IX. SAM LOVEL'S THANKSGIVING,	79
X. LITTLE SIS,	91
XI. SAM LOVEL'S BEE-HUNTING,	104
XII. IN THE SHOP AGAIN,	110
XIII. THE FOX HUNT,	116
XIV. NOAH CHASE'S DEER-HUNTING,	125
XV. THE HARD EXPERIENCE OF MR. ABIJAH JARVIS,	132
XVI. THE COON HUNT,	141
XVII. IN THE SUGAR CAMP,	149
XVIII. INDIANS IN DANVIS,	158
XIX. THE BOY OUT WEST,	167
XX. BREAKING UP,	172
XXI. THE DEPARTURE,	180
XXII. THE WILD BEES' SWARM,	185

UNCLE LISHA'S SHOP.

I.

THE SCHOOL MEETING IN DISTRICT 13.

For a week before the first Tuesday in the April of a certain year half a lifetime ago, the battered door of the shabby old school-house in District 13 of the township of Danvis bore a conspicuous patch of white paper among its scratches, bruises, and awkwardly carved initials. Some wayfarers knew at first sight what this early spring blossoming of the school-house door heralded; those who did not or hoped that it might advertise a "slayth o' hand show," or "a 'stronermy lectur'," or "temp'unce meetin'," found upon examination that it warned the "legil voters in school meeting in Dist. 13 in the town of Danvis to mete in the school house in sd. dist. on Tuesday evening, Aperil 3," etc.

Accordingly on the evening named in the warning, as the dismal landscape of the season grew dim in the twilight, the little building was illuminated by four candles, and the cracked, rusty stove glowed with fervent heat, for the committee and the "deestrick clark" had not been negligent of their duty, and having lighted the candles and the fire, now sat gazing thoughtfully, or with absence of thought, at the stove while they waited the coming of their neighbors. Presently, announcing their arrival with more than needful stamping and scraping of boots, there entered nearly all the legal voters of the district and almost as many boys, for without the presence of this non-voting but not altogether silent element, no school meeting had ever yet been held in District 13. Uncle Lisha Peggs, the cordwainer, was there, and Solon Briggs, the man of big if not weighty words, and Joseph Hill, and his aged sire whom Ethan Allen had assisted in the capture of Ticonderoga, and who had fought at Hubbardton and Bennington, and had ever since been ready to take a hand in any fight, whether of words or deeds. There were also present Samuel Lovel, the hunter, and his companion Drive, the hound, who took now no active part in the proceedings, but got himself under the stove and toasted his gaunt ribs with exceeding comfort while he bided his time. Loud and forthputting, there was Beri Burton, an uncouth giant, who had not long been a resident, having moved into the township from no one knew where, and who had the air of being burdened with a grievance and the malodor of "spilin' for a fight." Gran'ther Hill set his toothless jaws as he rested his chin upon his cane, and glowered at him as he could not have done more savagely at his ancient bitterest enemies, the Tories and Indians. Antoine Bassette, the Canadian, attended the meeting, not a voter, but interested as a furnisher of scholars, for every year was added one more black-polled, bare-footed toddler to his dusky brood that came jabbering along the dusty summer road to the old school-house.

Joel Bartlett, "clark of the deestrick," was a staid Quaker, whose mouth was made up for a whistle that the strictness of his religious views had never permitted him to utter, and he wore a wide-brimmed hat always abroad and much at home, and almost as constantly as this and the pucker of his lips, a coat supposed to be somewhat like that of George Fox, the founder of his sect. " Sammule," he said, when after sitting some time in silence his attention was attracted by the hound's yelping and pawing the air in pursuit of a shadowy fox on the hills of dreamland, " thy dawg appears kind 'er lanky, 's 'ough he hedn't wintered fust-rate. Thee feeds him, I hope?"

" Feed 'im !" said Sam, indignant at such an imputation on his treatment of his friend. " The' hain't a day goes over Drives's head 'at he don't hev a johnny-cake baked for 'im, an' he gits it, too. The trouble with Drive is, he's ben a preachin' raound hum all winter, a prophet 'thaout honor in his own country, ye know, an' not much profit to his marster. Mebby you've hearn him holdin' forth on Hawgs Back an' raound. He's got kinder thin duin' so much for so little, for he ain't no hirelin' minister, an' don't git nothin' but his board for his sarvices. Tow-ward the latter eend o' nex' month, Fif' month, I'm a goin' to start him off for yearly meetin', to New York or Newport, an' if he don't fat up there, I'm a goin' to git him recommended, an' hev 'im git a consarn to go on a visit to Friends to the east'ard. Ef that don't git 'im in good trim, I'll disown 'im, for he can't 'preciate blessin's, an' hain't fit to be a member 'mong Friends."

" Wal, Sammule," said Joel, with a twinkle in his eyes, " if thy dawg has ben a preachin' anything weighty, I'm afeared his marster's ears hes been closed, an' I think he better continner a sowin' the seed to hum, an' if the graound is barrern keep a harrerin' of it in."

The men laughed, and the boys snickered in the dark corners, and Joel, rising and looking around, said, " I think everybody is present 'at's 'xpected, an' perhaps the meetin' might as well becalled t' odder. Friends 'll please come t' odder."

All but himself took off their hats, and the whish of the boys' whispering ceased while he slowly read the warning, stooping to the nearest candle while he followed his forefinger along the lines. This ended, he said, "The fust thing is to choose a mawdrator. Will some friend please nomernate?"

"I nomernate Solon Briggs," said Sam Lovel, promptly, and "I secont the motion," some one else said as promptly. Then Joel proclaimed that Solon Briggs was "nomernated and seconted as mawdrator, an' them 'at favors him will say aye," and there was a small thunder of ayes.

"The contrayry-minded will say no," and only Beri Burton growled no.

"You hev made chice of Solon Briggs to sarve you as mawdrator," Joel announced, and Solon took his seat beside the clerk.

"In consumin' this persition," he said, slowly rising, and as slowly grinding his palms together, "to which I was chose unomynous without only one disseminatin' voice, I du it a hopesin' 'at this meetin' will cornduck itself becomin' an' harmonous an' proprietory; an' that them 'at is in the mynority will feel as content to be minoritorious as them 'at is in the may-jority will be to be majoritorious. An' we will naow perceed to transack business. The fust thing on the progerammy is to eleck a clark. Please nomernate a clark."

"I guess," said Uncle Lisha, scraping the wax off his left thumb with the nail of his right forefinger, and rolling it into pellets which he dropped upon the floor, " I guess 'at we'd better hev Joel. He's taown clark an' clark of his meetin', an' ben deestrick clark this ever so long, an' so he's got uster bein' clark. I nomernate Joel." Joel's nomination was seconded, and he was elected.

"The nex' thing," said Solon, "on the progerammy —or things—is a committee, one, tu, or three, to sarve as committee for the pursuin' year."

"Bein' 'at the' 's some," said Joseph Hill, propping himself into a half-standing position with his hands on the desks each side of him, " 'at thinks we'd better not go t' the expense o' hirin' of a man, but better kinder git along wi' a woman teacher this summer, an' the' 's some 'at don't, perhaps we'd better hev a committee 'at does or don't think so. F' my part, I d' know 's it makes much diffunce to me. I sh'ld like to hev a good teacher cheap, or a cheap teacher, an' hev him—her—it—a good one. I d' know 's I care much which sect the teacher is. I move 't we hev a man—or a womern."

"We do' wan' no school-mom!" roared Beri Burton; "Gol dum school-mom!"

"Afore we go any furder," said Joel Bartlett, rising and laying aside his hat, " I feel it borne in upon me to caution friends agin givin' away to their passions, an' to try an' conduck themselves with proper regard o' one 'nother's feelin's. Bein' 'at we haint all o' one mind, we can't expeck to be all on us suited; an' them 'at haint mus' try an' bear their disapp'intment, an' them 'at is mus' try an' not kerry 'emselves too high-headed." As he went on he unwittingly set his words to the dolorous tune to which the movings of his spirit went forth to those of his own belief on First-day and Fifth-day meetings.

"An', beloved friends, we must all on us, them 'at is up an' them 'at is daown, indivor for to—ah—be charitable an' kind an' forgivin', one untu another. A speakin' for myself, I can say that I think a suitable young womern 'ould arnswer aour purpose very well for the summer, as well as bein' more equinomical—"

"Thar!" cried Beri Burton, springing up like a gigantic jack-in-a-box, and mumbling his words as if they were so many hot potatoes, "thar, Misser Bartlutt, we do' wan' hear no more your dum blob; we do' wan' no school-mom, I tell ye. Had un las' summer, didn't us, an' what kin' er teacher was her? Why, noons an' art' school, an' boys aout an' gals aout fo'noon an' art'noon, the' was a feller—won't call no names—'at uster come to school-haouse, 'n' him an' school mom 'ld go daown inter medder strawberrin'. School-mom 'ld rub strawbers on 'er cheeks an' that 'ere feller 'ld buss 'em off! Gol dum such school-mom! Then 'cy 'd come up ter school-haouse, an' that 'ere feller 'ld git a board an' run it through the fence, an' school-mom 'ld git ont' one end on 't an' he'd get ont' tother, an' then they'd go teeter-tawter, teeter-tawter! Gol dum such school-mom. Do' wan' no more on 'em!"

"Ef I could on'y a hed that 'ere big heathin a front on me to Hubbar'ton or Bennin'ton," said Gran'ther Hill in a hoarse, whistling voice, "a-painted an' feathered, er dressed up in a red cut, he wouldn't a-ben a-troublin' 'on us to-night, he wouldn't."

"Ef I'd ha' knowed," retorted Beri, "'at this was a goin' to be a resurruction, stiddy a reg'lar school meetin', I'd ha' tooted up some o' my fo'fathers, or dug 'em up, an' brung 'em along to vote agin ye, ye ol' onburied cuss."

"Odder! Odder!" called Solon.

"Forefathers!" sneered Sam Lovel. "Ye never hed none, 'n' 'f ye hed the'y be 'shamed o' yer com'p'ny. I say odder, tu. He's same 's a skeeter to me. I don't care nothin' 'baout his bitin', but I do hate his cussed yowlin'."

"Jozeff!" commanded the ancient warrior, "you kinder stiddy me on my laigs so 's 't I c'n run my cane through that Hessian's in'ards!"

"Wal, naow, no, father, I guess I wouldn't, not 'f I was you," said his peaceable-minded son, "seem 's 'ough I wouldn't. 'F you sh'ld kill him, you'd git hung, 'n' that 'ould be turrible disgraceful for a man o' your years, an' one 'at's hed such 'scapes from Ticonderoge an' Hubbar'ton an' Bennin'ton. An' if you didn't, he might lick both on us, for I haint so spry 's I was, an' that would be turrible onpleasant for us an' turrible gratyfyin' for him. I haint no mind to give him no sech satyfaction."

"Bah gosh!" screamed Antoine, springing to his feet and dashing his tasselled woollen cap upon the floor, "Ah'll mek it notion we ant have it no school, 'f 'e can' have it aout all a tam quarly, quarly! Ah'll mek it notion we ant have it no school, me!"

"Odder! Odder!" Solon shouted, in a stern voice, "you're aouten odder, Antwine."

"What for Ah'm aout norder, M'sieu Brigg, hein?"

"Why, Antwine, you haint a legle voter in school meetin', ye see, don't ye? It 'ould be a diabolishment of parloramentary rules to 'low you to vote or speak. Ye haint never ben nat'ralized, ye know."

"Wal, Ah don' care 'f Ah don' nat'ral lie, so much you do. Ah'll show you jes' many chillun for go school anyboddee, bah gosh! More of it all a tam, evree year, evree year. Ah guess Ahm's more norder you was, M'sieu Brigg. You be marree more as Ah was, an' don' have it on'y but one chillun, bah gosh!" and Antoine grasped the seat of his baggy trousers with both hands preparatory to jumping upon his cap.

"Good airth an' seas!" Lisha roared in a voice that made the cracked window-panes jingle, and brought down some crumbs of plastering from the ceiling. "What's the motter ails ye, all on ye? We never hed no sech cussed works afore to a school-meetin' sen I was ol' 'nough to go to one! Ann Twine! You seddown an' shet up yer dum Canuck head! What's the motter ails ye?"

"It all comes," said Solon, "o' hevin' this 'ere imported disturbin' elephunt in aour midst of us, which we didn't uster hev it prevariously before last year."

What might then have happened if something else had not presently happened will never be known.

The men were growing angrier, and the repeated calls to order by the moderator, the loud voices and warlike demonstrations of their elders had hushed the boys in the back seats to such silence as their exuberant spirits had seldom known. Pelatiah Gove was the biggest of them, and having ciphered to the rule of three, was, therefore, unless he chose to make his painful way farther up the hill of learning toward the temple of science pictured on the first page of the spelling-book, to be considered a graduate of the district school. He was old enough to begin to think of the past, but whether with any longing to recall it perhaps he could not himself quite tell. He sat in his old seat by the window, vainly trying to accommodate his longer grown legs to their old position, and studying the initials and unmeaning devices his jack-knife had carved in the noontimes and stolen moments of past winters. He contrasted the present turbulent sounds with the drowsy buzz of the flies on the windows in the summer days when he so longed to go a-fishing in the brook that shot its tantalizing glints through the stems and shadows of the alders, and he turned his head to the window and looked toward the brook in a dreamy way. There seemed not much in that direction now to tempt one away from the warmth of the school-house, only that its atmosphere was becoming a little too warm, and if there was really to be what Pelatiah called "a reg'lar carummux," he, being a lover of peace, would rather not be present.

But something caught his abstracted gaze. He rubbed the dusty pane and put a hollowed hand on either side of his face, and, looking intently, counted one, two, three, four dark objects moving slowly across the dingy snow and dun dead grass of the fields, revealed with dim distinctness in the clouded moonlight. After a long look—though it was only a minute—to verify his first suspicion, he jumped to his feet, in his tangled haste almost tearing the desk from its place, shouting:

"'Coons! 'coons! four on 'em a-crossin' the road! Come on, all on ye! Here, Drive, sic 'em!" and made a dash for the door, shouting as he went, and emphasizing his calls with the thump! thump! of his heavy boots. "'Coons! come, Drive!" and Drive came suddenly out of dreamland and shot through the open door in hot eagerness for game more tangible than the phantoms of his sleep.

Pelatiah and the hound were followed in a mad rush by every one but the moderator and the clerk. These two stood aghast at the sudden breaking up of the meeting, and as Solon heard the shouts of the men and boys, and the baying of the deep-voiced hound coming fainter and fainter as they sped across the fields in pursuit of their quarry, he said, turning to his unmoved colleague, "The quorum has absquaterlated, an' I pernounce this meetin' is a-journed, Simon Dyer!"

And so he and Joel put out the lights and made the fire safe, and themselves went out. As they paused listening on the doorstep, with a human curiosity that neither the dignity of office nor the precepts of a stern religion could quite restrain, the voices of the men and boys of the pursuing party were hushed, and there was heard only the steady, insisting baying of the hound, now evidently not moving any farther away, nor moving at all.

"I ruther guess," said Joel, with his best ear turned toward the sound, and his mouth more tightly puckered for the unvoiced whistle, "I ruther guess the dawg has treed 'em, onless he's preachin' to Sammule. Don't thee think we'd better go an' see, Solon?"

II.

UNCLE LISHA'S SPRING GUN.

UNCLE LISHA PEGGS was the owner of a small farm lying so near the Green Mountains that his wood-lot was on a westering slope of one of their spurs, and the "black growth" of balsam and spruce crept down to the upper edge of the sugar-bush. His acres were too few to keep him steadily employed in their tillage, and so, in slack times, as well as in evenings and rainy days, he mended the boots and shoes of his neighbors, and was sometimes persuaded, as a special favor, to exercise the craft to the extent of building a pair of leathern conveniences. These productions could not be praised for their beauty, for the builder did not hold greatly to snug fits. If the sole of the wearer's foot set fairly on the inner sole of the boot and there were two or three points of contact with the uppers, his ideal of a perfect fit was realized.

He "'callated his stogies 'ould turn water like a cabbage-leaf if you gin 'em a dost o' taller or mushrat ile onct a week, an' wear julluk iron, an' when a feller onct got 'em broke they sot dreffle easy"—all of which was true, and especially the dreadfulness of the easiness.

One Sunday, late in summer time, when the sun shone hot from a brassy sky through a smoky haze that blurred the shadows' edges, and the grass was slippery with drought, and the locust gave voice to the parching heat, Uncle Lisha had performed the duty of church attendance, smoothing his way through it with a comfortable nap, and had eaten his Sunday dinner. He was now taking another nap in his " Windsor chair," a tilt on the stoop, his head and face smotheringly protected from the flies by the broad " bendinah hankercher," used only on Sundays, at weddings, funerals and county fairs. At last an exploring fly found his way under the edge of this expanse of dotted red silk, and got so far on his tour of discovery as the entrance of one of the caverns in the mountain of Lisha's nose, into which he was suddenly drawn by a sort of whirlwind, whereupon ensued a commotion which must have seemed to him at least an earthquake or a tornado. He was cast forth by a tremendous blast, the silken canopy was blown away, the chair came down on its forelegs with a bang that awakened Aunt Jerusha on her decorous patchwork couch in the darkened bedroom, the cat from her siesta, and set the fowls to cackling.

Of course Uncle Lisha was broad awake, and looking in to tell Aunt Jerusha that "the darn'd flies wouldn't let a feller sleep, an' he guessed he'd gwup an' see how the corn looked," rammed the bandana into the chamber of his bell-crowned beaver, as if loading a cannon, and then putting his head in for a ball, held across lots in his shirt-sleeves, his Sunday boots creaking soberly among the fading daisies of the pasture, and clattering against them a jerky tattoo. He forded, dry-footed, Stony Brook, now more stony than watery, and went through the corner of the sugar-bush, where the giant trees were healing their spring wounds in the summer sunshine, and past the silent shanty hovering its sap tubs and the upturned potash kettle, with squirrels and mice for housekeepers at this season.

Beside this lay the two acres of corn, the long leaves rolled by the heat into slender spikes, making the rows indeed "spiky ranks of maize," between which the pumpkins trailed their dark vines overhung by their own drooping leaves, pigeon grass and rag-weed, with here and there a yellowing globe shining through the rank growth, but not yet so bright as the golden chalices of late blossoms out of which the bees were drinking honey. The pollen of the tassels powdered the leaves, and the fray of silk at the end of the ears was turning from pale green to brown, showing that the kernels were set and well on in the milk and would soon begin to glaze in the furnace of August. In spite of the dry weather, the promise of a crop was very comforting to Uncle Lisha, till as he wandered through the rustling rows he came to the upper edge of the field nearest the dark woods, so near that their balsamic odors spiced the cloying sweetness of the corn-blossoms.

Here had been havoc. Stalks were torn and trampled down, ears stripped and munched and trodden into the earth as if a herd of swine had been at large among them.

"'Coons!" cried Uncle Lisha, as at first he stood aghast. "Darn'd if I don't get Sam Lovel to come up here with his hound to-night!—no, to-morrer night."

Then as his eye caught in the mellow soil the imprint of a clawed foot as big as his hand, he started with something like alarm. "Good airth and seas! it's a cussed bear! Yes," he said, as he plucked a tuft of long dark fur from the thorns of a blackberry by the fence, "it's a cussed bear!" Then, as he remembered the day, he apologized to his Sunday clothes—"Wall, he *is* a cussed bear! Why couldn't he a' eat blackberries, 'stead a spilin' ten bushels o' corn. Dutten corn, tew, none o' your nasty Tucket! Gol darn 'im, I'll set a spring gun for him to-night—no, to-morrer night!" And he set his face homeward, full of wrath and news, bearing in his hands a tuft of bear's fur and a munched ear of corn, in proof of the righteousness of the one and the truth of the other.

Monday forenoon was spent by him in warning his neighbors that he was about to set a spring gun, so that coon hunters and cross-lot travellers might not run into danger in his cornfield; and the afternoon was devoted to rigging the deadly contrivance.

First he loaded his ancient piece, which when set upright was taller than himself, with the old military charge, a ball and three buckshot on top of half his palmful of powder; then bearing the gun and his axe to the edge of the cornfield, he cut two stout stakes three feet long, which he drove into the ground about four feet apart, and then split the tops downward far enough to allow the gripe of the gun to be forced into the cleft of the first and the barrel into that of the second, so that the line of fire should be according to established rule—" at the hayth of the outside bone of a feller's knee." Close to and opposite the lock he drove another stake, on top of which he fixed a short lever with one end resting against the front of the trigger. To the other end, when the work was completed, was attached a line of elm bark, rubbed with earth to dull its too conspicuous whiteness and stretching out sixty or seventy feet beyond the gun muzzle, running at intervals through cleft stakes, wedged to keep them from pinching it.

When Uncle Lisha's task was done, and he straightened his long bent back with his palms and gave a last critical look at his infernal machine, he could see no reason why it should not do its deadly work if the bear would do his part. So toward sundown he primed the gun and, setting it at full cock, left it to guard the cornfield. Hoping to get a booming report that should tell of the death of the spoiler, he hardly got into his accustomed heavy sleep till midnight, but was not awakened from it by any sound till cockcrow.

Then, when the rayless sun was rising like a red moon above the ridge of the mountain, he went to the cornfield and found everything undisturbed, no more corn destroyed, and the old gun asleep with beads of dew on its rusty barrel. He made it harmless for the day by brushing the priming out of the pan and setting it at half-cock.

"Las' night want his night," he said, "but he'll come to-night, see 'f he don't!" and went home.

Toward nightfall he put the spring gun on guard again. As in the gloaming he leaned over the "do'yárd" fence, smoking a meditative pipe, with his eastern ear unconsciously cocked toward the cornfield, he became aware of an intermittent glow a furlong down the lonely road that outshone the flashing of the fireflies. It was somebody's pipe, and as it drew nearer its dim light revealed the features of Antoine Bassette, a self-exiled Canadian "patriot," who had fought and fled with Papineau, and had taken shelter here, safe from the lion's paw even in the edge of the eagle's nest, where he was hatching out into an American citizen, chipping the shell with brave pecks at the speech and customs of Yankee land. Thus far in his life's pilgrimage he had shuffled along in moccasins, but as he drew near to naturalization he aspired to boots, which, having been bespoken and duly measured for, were the cause of his visit to Uncle Lisha.

"Bushoo, musheer," said Lisha, airing his French in the twilight.

"Bon soir, monsieur," politely responded Bassette, and then with more faith in his own English, poor as it was, than in Lisha's French, good as its owner thought it: "Prob'ly you got dem boot done, Onc' Lasha, don't it? Wal, prob'ly it an't. Wal, Ah don't care, you get heem done fore soon, prob'ly. One man tole me bear heat mos' all up you corn, Onc' Lasha, an' you goin' catch heem wid gawn. Dat so, Onc' Lasha, hein! You tink it bear, Onc' Lasha? Wal, ah guess it Ba'tlett's hol saow, me. Sacre cochon! heat all ma patack. Daam hole pig like dat! You gat good gawn, Onc' Lasha? Ah spose so, prob'ly, good gawn keel bear? Da a no bear you co'nfeel. Ba'tlett's hol saow. Ah hope you gawn ketch heem, me. You gat dat boots did, Onc' Lasha?"

And not till now did Lisha find a chance to answer that they were not done, and that he was sure it was not neighbor Bartlett's hog that had done the mischief in the cornfield, for he had seen plainly the tracks of a bear and had found fur such as never grew on swine.

The boots were so near completion that a half-hour's work would make them ready for the torture of the poor Canuck.

"Come in, Ann Twine, come in, an' I'll finish 'em up to rights." So saying, Uncle Lisha led the way into his little shop and lighted the candle which, stuck in the end of a jointed wooden sconce, illumined his nightly labors. Then he deliberately donned his leather apron, lowered himself into the polished leathern seat of his shoe-bench, set his iron-rimmed, owl-eyed spectacles astride his nose, fished out the boots from a clutter of clumsy lasts, broad slabs of sole leather, rolls of cowhide and sheepskin, gave his long shoe-knife a rasping on the peculiar, coarse, gritty stone used only by shoemakers, and was ready for work, or would have been if the sharp knife had not reminded him of a story which he began to tell, while the edge of the knife and the boot, held between his knees, shared, by turns, his admiring glances.

"Ann Twine, when my father lived in C'net'cut he knowed a man 'at had a shoe knife julluck that 'at was the cutest thing to cut bread with anybody ever see, so't they useter send for the shoemaker to go to tarverns when the' was trainin's and to housen when the' was gret weddin's, an' such carummuxes, jest a puppus to cut the bread. Onct the' was a gret shearin' to Colonel Leavenworth's 'at kep a thousand sheep, an' had twenty shearers an' big doin's genally, an' they sent for him to—"

But he did not finish his story that night, for just then the heavy air was torn by a loud report, so startling in the midst of the outer stillness that had been broken only by the steady creak of the crickets, that it might remind one of the signal-gun of some savagely-beleaguered block-house of the olden time, and 'Tater Hill hurled back an echo like an answering gun from another fort, and Hog's Back another, and mingling with the swelling and dying reverberations was an angry yell as of attacking Indians.

"Good airth an' seas!" cried Uncle Lisha, scattering his exclamations, his spectacles, and the boot from the shoe-bench to the dooryard gate, as he rushed out, brandishing his knife.

"Come on, Ann Twine, come on, I've got him!"

He was half way across the pasture before Antoine decided to follow him, and the Canadian barely kept the valorous old Yankee in sight in the hazy moonlight as he stumbled across the stony field and splashed through the brook and quite lost him among the shadows of the maples, but found him again in the cornfield just in time to see him charge upon a writhing black object, the bear, sorely hit with the ounce ball and buckshot. The fray was short, the bear sank out of it in a limp heap and his conqueror crept out of it, groaning:

"Oh, Ann Twine, be you here?" he gasped. "The dummed etarnal critter's tore all my insides out, but I've gathered up the best on 'em an' I'm goin' to try to git home with 'em."

As he became more clearly revealed to the terrified Frenchman in the hazy light of the harvest moon, he was seen to be stooping painfully along, bearing some burden in his gathered apron.

"Oh, sacre! sacre! sacre! Da's too bad, Onc' Lasha, too bad, too bad! Oh, sacre! Bah gosh, sacre!" He had seen nothing so terrible in the Papineau war. "Oh, what Ah do, Onc' Lasha, what Ah do?"

"You can't help me here none, Ann Twine, but you out fu' the house an' git onter the hoss an' put fur the darkter. Mabby he c'n stuff 'em back so they'll answer for a spell."

Antoine, with a face whiter than the moon that shone above him, sped across the fields at a pace which had distinguished the close of his military career. He shot himself into the kitchen of the little farm-house and gave placid Aunt Jerusha a dreadful shock with the dire tidings that "Onc' Lasha keel bear an' bear keel heem! Hole man dead an' bringen' hissif home in hees aprum! Ah go for doctah rat off!"

The next minute he was in the barn, saddling the old horse, and five minutes later went clattering down the road at a lumbering gallop toward the doctor's, five miles away.

Poor Aunt Jerusha went hurrying across the pasture to give her wounded lord such succor as she could, with an unwonted sickness at her stout heart. It was a sufficient sign of her trepidation and alarm that she had forgotten to put on her sun-bonnet. Half way across the field, Lisha became discernible against the dull whiteness of the mouse ear and everlasting of the sterile hillside. As they approached each other, he seemed indeed to be bringing himself home in his apron, as the Frenchman had said, stooping over a burden in that garment which was gathered in both his hands.

"Oh, father, be you dead?" sobbed Aunt Jerusha, in a voice strangely mixed of shrill and deep tones.

"No, mother, I ain't dead; but I guess I'm goin' to be. The 'tarnal critter has tore me all to pieces! My heart an' lights an' stummerk is inside yet, but I guess he's scooped out all the rest on 'em."

"Oh, what kin I do for ye, father; what kin I do?" cried the wife. "Antwine's gone lickaty split arter the darkter, an' 't can't be long 'fore he'll come. I do' know as I could git 'em back right if I tried, but I'll try 'f ye say so, father."

"No, mother," Lisha answered, weakly; "you can't do nothin', only keep along with me, jist as ye allers have, Jerushy," he added, with a tremulous tenderness in his voice that reminded her of its tones when she was young and fair Jerusha Chase, and he came courting on the Sunday nights, left forty years behind in their plodding journey.

So they went slowly homeward, she, when they came to

the fences, making a way for him to pass through. When at last they got home, the good old wife put him and his burden tenderly to bed in clothes and apron, and then, with the housewifely instinct strong upon her even in the midst of trouble, put things "to rights" for the doctor's visit, and as quietly as possible awaited that event.

Some neighbors to whom Antoine had scattered out crumbs of the burden of news as he journeyed toward the doctor's, came dropping in to offer their help with the ready kindness of our primitive communities. But there was nothing for them to do. Two or three of the oldest women sat in the little bedroom where Aunt Jerusha watched beside her husband, whom she dared not doubt was soon to leave her alone in this end of the world, for their only son had settled in "the 'Hio," then almost at the other end of the world. The other women sat primly against the walls of the "square room," some telescoping their sun-bonnets together and magnifying in whispers the latest neighborhood gossip.

The men lounged in the doorways or against the side of the house and dooryard fence, and told in low voices their experience with bears and discussed this most recent and tragic one.

"Uncle Lisha hedn't fit bears much," said Samuel Lovel, a tall farmer who loved hunting more than farming; "'f he hed he wouldn't a-tackled one with a shoe-knife."

"Wal," said Tom Hamlin, another hunting farmer, "it don't somehow seem noways fair t' set spring guns and traps and such for varmints, 'thout it's skunks an' mink an' mushrats. I'd rather shute one bear 'n' t' trap ten. They ha' no more instinc' about a trap 'n' a skunk hes!"

"Wal," drawled Joseph Hill, "skunks hes outstink!—seems 's 'ough they hed."

"But then," apologized Joel Bartlett, "thee sees he was a-eatin' all Uncle Lisha's corn, 'n' the'd got to be suthin' did. I should feel bore aout in killin' a bear any way I could—if I hed to pizen him."

"That would spile the skin," objected Joseph Hill, with an eye to the main chance, "'n' I d' know but 'twould the ile; sartainly 'twould the meat."

"Dot rot bear's meat," Tom Hamlin said; "I'd jes' 's soon eat snake's meat!"

"Wal," remarked Joseph Hill, "I've hearn o' folks 'at liked snake's meat. I'd a leetle druther hev bear. It all depends on how a feller was brung up, 'n' we never hed no snakes cooked 't aour haouse—that is, not 's I remember on."

"Wonder 'f Uncle Lisha's bear's fat?" queried a thrifty man. "'F he is 't 'ill be quite a help to the widder. Bear's ile is wuth suthin' consid'able."

"It's a hopesin' the' haint a-goin' tu be no widder," said Sam Lovel; "we can't let Uncle Lisha go yit awhile —but there!" exclaimed the tall hunter, unlooping himself from the fence, "why haint we thought to go an' fetch the bear hum 'stead a-loafin' round here duin' nothin'? Come on, men; git a' axe to cut a pole an' a rope to tie his laigs together — no, the line of the gun 'll do for that."

And so, the axe found, a half dozen of them started across the field and faded out of sight long before their voices were drawn beyond hearing.

The doctor had been aroused from his slumbers by Antoine's loud summons to "Come up to Onc' Lasha.

Bear tore his eenside all off, an' he don' gat ma boot done, mos'."

The first of the small hours found the rough but kindly old mediciner at Lisha's door before the bearers had returned with the dear-bought spoil.

"Now, come in here with me, you two chaps," he said, selecting a couple of stout hearts, " and bring each on ye a candle. Well, Lisha," looking at his patient intently and examining his pulse, "you don't 'pear so very bad off. Guess we can fix you up for another bear fight yet ! Now, men, hold the lights," and he put on his spectacles, rolled back his cuffs and turned down the folds of the leather apron. He carefully touched and closely inspected for a moment what was disclosed, then his face flushed angrily, and the candle-bearers were horrified to see him gather up the trailing mass in both hands and hurl it across the room, roaring :

"You confounded old fool ! these all belong to the bear !"

Though Lisha had received some ugly scratches, he had suffered no serious injury, and was able next day to finish Antoine's boots. And in consideration of his services in the old man's hour of sore trial he was made happy, until he had worn them a day, by having them given him outright.

III.

IN UNCLE LISHA'S SHOP.

AFTER his adventure with the bear, Uncle Lisha Peggs's shop became more than ever what it had long been, a sort of sportsman's exchange, where, as one of the fraternity expressed it, the hunters and fishermen of the widely scattered neighborhood met of evenings and dull out-door days "to swap lies." Almost every one had a story to tell, but a few only listened and laughed, grunted, or commented as the tale told was good, bad or of doubtful authenticity. And so one October evening, as the rising hunter's moon was streaking the western slopes with shadows of evergreen spires and long paths of white moonlight, Uncle Lisha's callers began to drop in by ones and twos. The first comer got the best seat, the broken-backed chair, the next the second best, so accounted, the chair with three legs, though the occupant had to give so much thought to the keeping of his balance, that he sometimes tumbled to the floor when the laugh came in. The later comers had the choice of seats on a roll of sole leather, the cold box-stove, or a board laid across the tub in which Lisha soaked his leather, and the latest the floor, with the privilege of lying at length upon it or setting their backs against the plastered wall. So were disposed a half score of the old cordwainer's neighbors, thus far doing little but smoke, chew, and silently watch Lisha as he hammered out, shaped and pegged on the tap of a travel-worn boot as intently as if they were taking lessons in the craft, when Antoine Bassette entered with a polite "Good evelin, Onc' Lasha; good evelin, all de zhontemans." Then as he looked about he drew forth from one pocket his short black pipe, from another his knife, with which he scraped out the pipe and emptied it on the stove hearth, then he got out from another a twist of greenish-black tobacco, and whittling off a charge and grinding it between his palms, filled and lighted his pipe at Lisha's candle with such sturdy pulls that the little dip seemed likelier to be quenched than to longer "shine like a good deed in a naughty world."

"Git aout! ye dummed peasouper," Lisha shouted, after pounding his fingers instead of a peg in the uncertain light, "you'll hev us all in total moonlight fust ye know! Take a match er a splinter an' light yer pipe like white folks, stiddy suckin' my candle aout. Don't ye know what the feller said 'at was goin' t' be hung in ten minutes, when they gin him a candle t' light his pipe with? He says, says he, 'Gimme a match, if ye please, 'taint healthy t' light a pipe with a candle,' says he. Take keer 'f yer health, Ann Twine, f' that 'ere Canady Gov-'ner 'll want ye t' be wuth hangin', when he gits a holt on ye."

"Hah, naow, Onc' Lasha," said Antoine, "dat wus too bad faw you talk so to me. Who help you w'en dat bear keel you, hein?"

"Wal, yes," Lisha rejoined, "ye did help, sartin; the bear an' I done the fightin' an' you done the runnin'. You larnt how to du that in the Pap'neau war, an' ye larnt it well, Ann Twine; ye don't need no more lessons."

"Wal, Ah do, seh. Ah wan' some bodee show me haow Ah run wid dem boot you mek me 'f Ah don' cah heem in mah han', an' den he pooty heavy. But, bah gosh! wa' heem on ma foots? Ah jus' leave wa' two stofe like dat. He be jus' so sof', jus' so not heavy."

"Haow d' ye 'spose any body could fit yer dummed Canuck feet arter ye'd wore souyaas* ever sen' ye was weaned, ker-splash, ker-spotter, till yer feet's wider'n they be long? You git ye some babeesh† an' I'll give ye tew sides o' sole luther, an' then ye can make ye some souyaas, 'n' then put on yer ole trouses 'at ye could carry a week's p'vision in the seat on, an' be a Canuck; ye can't be a 'Merican, no ways."

"Ah, Onc' Lasha! You pooty bad hole man. Haow you feel dat time you tink you dead? Wha' you tink you go? A'nt you sorry you don't was been mo' gooder? Wha' you tink you go, hein?"

"I do' know," Uncle Lisha slowly responded; "but I hoped I'd go where the' wa'n't no Canucks!"

"Dah! dah! Onc' Lasha; you so weeked no use talk to you," cried Antoine, when the laugh in which he joined had subsided; "'f you tole dat leet'ly story you beegin dat night, Ah won't said no mo'; you leave off rat in meedly w'en de bear shoot heself, an' you see Ah got so Yankee Ah mos' come dead 'cause Ah do' know de en' of it. Dat story, you know, 'bout man dat cut bread so fas' wid shoe-knife. You rembler?"

"Le' me see," said Lisha, scratching his head with his awl; "oh, yes, I remember! Wal, I s'pect that's a true story, Ann Twine, an' 'f I tell it ye got t' b'lieve it."

---

* Moccasins.   † Rawhide used for sewing moccasins.

"Oh, sartin, Onc' Lasha; Ah don' b'leeve you tole lie no more as Ah do; no, sah."

"Humph!" Lisha grunted. "I never knowed but one Canuck but what 'ould lie."

"An' dat was me, Onc' Lasha?"

"No, sir! He was a dead one! Wal, the' was a shoemaker 't lived in Connecticut, an' my father knowed him, 'at hed a knife julluk this"—holding up his longest knife—"the cutest thing t' cut bread with't ever was, but he wouldn't let nob'dy but his own self use it, so they use ter send fer him to all gret duins t' cut the' bread fer 'em. Wal, arter he'd ben a-cuttin' raoun' for three, fo' year, they sent fer him one July to go t' Colonel Leavenworth's gret shearin'. He kep' a thousan' sheep, an' hed twenty shearers, an' made a big splonto, 'wine in quart mugs an' strawb'ries rolled in cream,' he use ter brag about, but they wan't on'y pint mugs 'n not filled very often at that, an' the wine was cider, an' the' wan't more 'n tew strawb'ries apiece, 'n' they was dried apples. Wal, the shoemaker come with his knife keener 'n ever, an' the han's an' comp'ny hed all got washed up for dinner with the' clean clo's on, an' stood raound watchin' on him cut the bread, ker slice, ker slice, faster 'n a gal could pick up the slices, off 'm a loaf 't he hel' agin his breast. He done it so neat 't they cheered him, which he got kinder 'xcited, an' tried t' cut faster 'n ever, an' the next lick he gin the loaf he cut hisself clean in tew, an' the man 'at stood behind him clean in tew, an' badly waounded the next one. They sot tew an' stuck 'em together so 't they lived, but it spilte the shoemaker's bread-cuttin' business, an' he hed to go back to shoemakin' an' starvin', julluk me."

"Wal, sah, Onc' Lasha," cried Antoine, emphasizing every word with a gesture, "Ah b'lieve dat story, 'cause Ah promise, baht Ah tink 'twas 'cause you goin' tole it dat bear scrape you so bad. You see, sah, bear is send for punish bad folkses. An't you hear haow bear keel fawty-leetly boy 'cause dey call hol man he don' got no hair on top hees head of it—what you call heem—bal'? Ah spec' dey be nudder bear long 'fore soon for ketch hol man what tole such story, an' den tell Frenchman he don' lie honly w'en he dead!"

"Good airth an' seas!" Lisha roared, "I du believe one on 'em would hev the last word 'f he was deader 'n a door nail. Wal," he continued, as he put his tools in their places and took off his apron, "it's 'baout time 't honest folks was abed an' rogues locked aout, but you needn't hurry none 'baout goin' t' bed, Ann Twine."

Ten minutes later the shop was dark but for the patch of moonlight that shone in through the little window set longwise of the room, and the visitors scattered to their homes.

IV.

CONCERNING OWLS.

ONE night when the November wind was growling among the stunted firs that crest old " 'Tater Hill," already grizzly with more than one snowfall, the brotherhood of hunters and fishers, story-tellers and listeners came stumbling along the rough frozen roads and across the frosty fields to Lisha's shop. The little box-stove was no longer cold; its red jaws grinned defiance at approaching winter, and its cheeks blushed with a ruddier glow than the summer's rust had given them, and its warmth heightened the odors of tannin, wax and mouldy boots that always hold their own in the atmosphere of the cobbler's shop. The firing of the stove would have unseated two visitors if a couple of sap tubs with a board laid across them had not made room for twice as many, and this was now the coveted first place for the coldest comers to sit in and thaw out their chilled marrows and their wells of conversation. To this extent had Sam Lovel been warmed when he opened his lean jaws, and said with a sigh of pent-up satisfaction, "Ah, wal, Uncle Lisher, I ketched a-nuther bear t' day."

"Du tell!" said Lisha, drawing hard on the waxed ends with which he was closing up a ripped boot-leg. "Wal, Sam, was he 's heavy 's ole Cap'n Powerses hawg was? 'Killed tew hawgs terday,' says 'e, ' both on 'em good ones, but one on 'em was a sollaker, I tell ye—weighed ninety!' Was ye' bear's heavy 's that, Sam?"

"Wal," Sam asked, "haows three hund'ed an' seventy-seven? That's his heft ezackly."

"Real weight or guess weight?" some one asked.

"Why, real weight, 'f course, an' no guessin' 'baout it."

"Where 'd ye weigh him?"

"T' hum," Sam replied shortly.

"Sho!" sneered the doubter, "ye hain't got no scales nor bolances! Haow could ye weigh 'im t' hum?"

"Wal, naow, I did weigh 'im fair an' hones', an' he weighed jist ezackly what I tell ye. I c'n lift jist three hund'ed an' fifty paound, an' I couldn't lift him inter j-e-s-t twenty-seven paound. Naow 'f that don't make three hund'ed and seventy-seven, I hain't got no 'rethmytic."

A long young man, whose arms and shanks seemed to have lengthened beyond his means to keep them clothed, ventured to say as he looked admiringly upon his new buckskin mittens, too precious to be taken off his hands, but kept opening and closing and turning on them just before his eyes, "The's a painter a-hantin' on Hawg's Back, I du raly b'lieve; I hearn the gol darnedest yollupin' up there t'other night, julluk a womern a hollerin', 'n' I hollered, 'n' it arnswered, an' kep' comin' nigher, 'n' then I started my boots fer hum, I tell ye!"

"Sho! Sho! Peltier, you git aout!" Lisha roared, for he was apt to think it his exclusive right to see and hear all strange things first. "'Twan't nothin' but a big aowl, I bet ye!"

"'Twan't no aowl," cried Pelatiah, clapping his mittened palms together with a resounding smack; "'twas a annymill! Guess I know an aowl when I hear 'im!"

"Wal, mebby 'twas a lynk. A lynk 'll git up a c'nsid-'able 'f a skeery yowlin'. 'N' mebby 'twas tew ole tomcats a-fightin' up 't ye' west barn. D'ye ever hear, boys," Lisha continued, without waiting for any reply from Pelatiah, "baout Joel Bartlett's Irishmun 't he sent up int' the aidge o' the parster a-choppin' one day? Didn't ye, none on ye? Wal, up he went, and bimeby he come a-runnin' back scairt half ter death, an' hollerin' 'Murther! oh, murther! it's a painter I seen, sure 's me name's Pat Murphy!' 'Show!' says Joel, 'haow 'd he look, Partrick?'

"'Wal,' says Pat, 'he was yolly, sur, an' he had a long tail on 'im.'

"'Wal, naow, Partrick, wa'n't it aour ole yaller tomcat?'

"'Be gob, sur, it moight,' sez Pat, an' he lit his pipe an' went back to his choppin' 's contented 's if the' hedn't never been a painter in V'mont."

Pelatiah's panther being thus contemptuously disposed of, the conversation turned for a time to owls.

"Aowls," said Lisha, as he rolled a waxed end upon his aproned knee, "'ll make turable onairthly an' skeery noises, p'tic'ly big aowls, which the's more 'n one kind on 'em, hoot aowls, an' white aowls 'n' I d' know what aowls. I've hed 'em make my hair stan' right stret up, sen I was older 'n Peltier is, tew."

"Wal, I don't keer a darn what ye say," said Pelatiah, after breathing through the back of his right-hand mitten to assure himself for the hundredth time that it was genuine buckskin, "'twan't no aowl 't I heard, 'twas a annymill!

'F I hed me a rifle I'd go a-huntin' on 'im;'' but he could arouse no interest in his panther further than the offer from Jonas Gove of his rifle for half the bounty, if the panther was killed, or half a dollar a day for the use of the weapon, which was declined.

Tom Hamlin said that he had heard "a dozen gret aowls a-hootin' an' a-shoutin' as he come along."

"Yaas, Tawmus," said Solon Briggs, who was weather-wise as well as wise in other things, "so'd I, an' the's goin' to be some kind o' fallin' weather 'fore long, you see 'f the' hain't."

"Wal, yas," Tom assented, "most allus the' is arter they hoot so. Haow d' y' 'caount for it, Sole?"

"Waal, I'll tell ye, Tawmus. I've meddytated on 't c'nsid'able, an' my idee 's this"—crossing his legs and putting his right forefinger into the palm of his left hand—"D'ye ever have the rheumatiz?"

"Yas, I've hed 'em."

"'N' wa'n't they wus 'fore a storm?"

Tom nodded repeatedly, and said, "They was wus."

"Waal, naow then," Solon continued, "the aowls 't we hear is big aowls, an' nat'ally they're ol' aowls, 'n' they've got the rheumatiz, an' when the's a storm a-comin' on the rheumatiz begin to rack 'em, an' they holler aout. Hain't that re'son'ble naow, and"—looking around upon the company and bringing down his finger with a clinking smack upon his palm—"and phillysoffycable, so to speak?"

"P'haps," said Lisha, as he rasped his knife upon the sandstone, "someb'dy could tell us suthin' 'baout shootin' aowls; haow is it, Jozeff?" he asked, looking between his shaggy eyebrows and the top of his spectacles at a thick-set fellow who was taking his ease in a farther corner of the shop.

"Naow, Lisher," said Joseph, "you keep on tellin' yer stories an' lemme 'lone, if you please."

"Jozeff," said Lisha in a terrible voice, shaking his knife at the unwilling story-teller, "you tell 'baout ye shootin' the aowl, er I will!"

"Wal, then," said Joseph, slowly getting into a sitting posture, and knocking the ashes from his pipe, "I guess you'd make it wus 'n I would, 'n' so I'll tell it. Ye see, the' was a big aowl come, gol blast him, an' kerried off half a dozen, I d' know but more—no, mebbe baout that 'maount o' M'ri's chickins, an' I tole M'ri, I did, 't I'd fix him 'fore he knowed it. So next night, er I guess mebbe next night arter—one er t'other, anyhaow—I looked aout the winder, an' I seen him a-sittin' on a clo's pos', an' I got my gun, I did. M'ri open the winder kinder easy, an' I poked the gun aout an' onhitched on 'im; but somehaow the gun wa'n't loaded fur aowls, er I was too fas', er suthin, an' I never tetched 'im! Shot over, I s'pose—anyway, I thought I did. Wal, next Monday night when the clo's was all a-hangin' aout, he come agin, he did, an' sot on the same clo's pos'. I hed the ole gun all ready, an' M'ri open the winder agin, an' I run 'er aout, an' took dead aim a foot below th' aowl, fur says I to myself, says I, I won't overshoot this time, says I, an' I let flicker, an' I be darned if I didn't miss him, but, by gosh! I blowed my harnsome shirt 't hung right below 'im all to flinders. It tickled M'ri t' think 't I made sech a good shot, an' I spec' she tol' on it; I didn't, not fust, I don't b'lieve; 'n' Lisher, darn his ole picter, he got holt on it." When the laugh subsided,

Joseph added, "Wal, 'twa'n't a bear, 'n' he didn't tear my insides aout, if my shirt did git tore!"

Uncle Lisha tossed the mended boot to its owner, who sat nursing the stockinged foot to which it belonged, and laying aside his tools arose and took off his apron, which was a signal to his visitors to depart, and so they presently disappeared in the dim starlight of the November night.

V.

UNCLE LISHA'S COURTING.

Though in mid-day there was yet a hazy after-taste of the sweetness of Indian summer, the season was beginning to have a smack of winter in its night air. On such an evening, as the first star began to shine above the rounded peak of 'Tater Hill, Lisha rubbed the mist off a pane of his long, low shop window, and stooping his eye to it, peered out upon the darkening road. Out of the gloaming presently grew some dark shapes into men, the sound of whose footsteps and voices came a little before them. When they and others had entered and been welcomed by Lisha, he having lighted his pipe and taken some work in hand, declared " the meetin' open," and that they " was all ready to transact business." Little was said till some one remarked, " Pwheeew !" And then all became aware that an odor more pungent and powerful than those of leather and shoemaker's wax was pervading the atmosphere of the shop.

"Good airth an' seas!" cried Lisha, " I secont the motion! Le's all whew! Some on ye stepped on suthin' t'night, or somebody got skunk's ile to sell."

Each took a sniff of his neighbor till the source of the fragrance was traced to Pelatiah's corner, when he shamefacedly confessed that he " hed ben a-trappin' a leetle," but said in extenuation, " I sot fer mink. I hed one trap sot in a holler log over to Hillses' brook, with a ruster's head fer bait, an' when I went tu it yist'day, the trap was hauled int' the log. I pulled on the chain c'nsid'able stout, but it didn't le' go a bit, an' then I god daown on all fours an' peeked in to see what the matter was ailded it, an'—oh, gosh all Connet'cutt! My eyes hain't god done smartin' yit! I rolled an' I tumbled till I got to water, 'n' then I washed an' rubbed an' scrubbed till I c'ld see nuthin' 'sides stars and fire, an' then I went hum an' baried all them clo's, an' washed me in three waters an' smudged me with hemlock browse, an', gosh darn it all, I didn't 'spose I wa'n't all sweetened aout! 'F my comp'ny hain't 'greeable I'll dig fer hum."

"Sho!" Lisha shouted, with hearty politeness, "guess we c'n stan' it 'f you can! 'S fer me, I ruther like a leetle good fresh skunk parfum'ry. The's some 'at eats 'em"—rolling his eye toward a known mephitipophagist —"an' I sh'd think them 'at likes the taste would the smell. Furdermore, I'm beholden to skunks fer c'nsid'- able myself. Keep yerself comf'table, Peltier."

No one objected to Pelatiah's presence, and several asked Lisha how he was indebted to skunks for anything.

"Wal," said he, slowly scraping the sole of a boot with a bit of broken glass, while his thoughts went backward over the rough path of his life, "in the fust place, when I was a leetle chap they cured me o' croup with skunk's ile, which they gi'n it ter me spoo'ful arter spoo'ful, an' greesed my stomerk with it outside, tew. An' then arter I'd got growed up, skunk essence cured me of azmy. An' then—I don't scasely b'lieve I'd ha' ever got Jerushy 'f 't hed n't a been fer a skunk!"

After the "wal I swans," and "goshes," and "you

don't says,'' which this declaration called forth, there was a general demand for an explanation, and Lisha laid down his boot and glass, and devoted himself wholly to the telling of his story, with his elbows on his knees and locking and unlocking his waxy fingers as he talked, as if so he wove the woof of his tale.

" I never sot no gret on ole folks tellin' of what they'd did, or ben, or hed when 't they was younger, but when Jerushy was Jerushy Chase she was 'baout 's pooty a gal as c'ld be dug up in tew, three taowns, an' as smart and cap'ble, an' nat'lly she was sought arter, an' none the less 'cause her father was tol'able well off. When I begin a-sparkin' on her, I hed n't nothin' much but my tew hands, was a-workin' aout by the month for this one an' that one for six or eight months, an' I'd larnt to shoemake a leetle, so 's 't I ' whipped the cat '* winters, so ye see I was arnin' suthin' all the time, an' I wa'n't sech a humbly ole critter 's I be naow, so 's 't I stood jes 's good a chance as any o' the fellers, till bimeby the' come a chap to teach aour deestrick school, a college feller f'm Middlebury. He was a clever creeter, an' smart, an' good-natured an' hahnsome, c'ld rastle like a bear, 'n' sing like a boblink, 'n' wore hahnsome clo's every day, so all the gals 'most was a-ravin' an' a-rarin' arter him. Jerushy wa'n't, though, an' that made him the faster and fircer arter her. An' so arter awhile his pooty talk an' hahnsome clo's an' all them college things begin to work on her, 'n' she git so 't she'd mos' lives I would n't come Sunday nights as not.

---

* " Whipping the cat " is working from house to house at shoemaking or tailoring, as was a common custom in old times.

"So it run along till tow-ward the middle o' sugarin', she a-favorin' him a leetle mor'n me of the tew, an' the' was goin' to be a gret sugarin' off to Hillses, 'n' most everbody hed a *in*vite. I went 'n' ast Jerushy to go 'long with me, 'n' she said she ' didn't know ; guessed she'd go 'long with the one 'at come arter her fust.' Thinks, says I, Mr. Schoolmarster, 'f you get to Uncle Chase's 'fore I du, you'll hafter pull foot for it lively. So 'long in the middle o' the art'noon I got my chores all done up, an' dressed me an' put off. I put 'crost lots, 'n' I hedn't got fur when darned if I didn't see that 'tarnal schoolmarster jest a-goin' int' the aidge o' Meeker's Woods, pintin' for Uncle Chase's, 'n' nearer tu it 'n' I was. I doubled my jumps an' got there, an' tole Jerushy I'd got there fust 'n' she'd got to go 'long with me. She kinder hung off, lookin' outen the winder every onct an' awhile, but nary a schoolmarster ! An' so bimeby she got rigged up, an' off we went, an' had a gret carummux to the sugarin'. She kep' a-sythin' an' a-peekin' fer a spell, but nary a schoolmarster, an' then she got desput jolly, 'n' made more fun 'n the hull toot on 'em. Goin' hum in the moonshine, I ast her to jine me in a sugarin' for life, an' 'fore we got to the chips in the do'yard she 'greed she would, an' here we be ! Me on this 'ere shoebench, an' she," lifting his voice and pointing a waxy forefinger at the door that opened into the kitchen, " an' she a-peekin' through the crack o' that 'ere door !" The door squeaked suddenly to, and the wooden latch clicked rather spitefully.

"Wal," said one disappointed auditor, breaking the short ensuing silence, " wha'd all that hev ter du with a skunk ?"

"Oh, nuthin' much," said Lisha, " only ye see that

feller was a-shovin' 'long the best he knowed, through the woods in a wood road, an' fust thing he run spat ont' a skunk aout takin' a walk. The skunk wouldn't run, an' he wouldn't, an' it turned aout con'try to scriptur. The battle *was* to the strong, an' the race *was* to the swift. The schoolmarster smelt loud 'nough to fill a forty-acre lot, an' so the' wa'n't no schoolmarster t' Chases' nor t' the sugarin'-off, nor t' the school in that deestrick that spring, nor nothin' left on him in the deestrick but his parfume. So, ye see, a skunk hed suthin' t' du with his scaseness, which I c'nsider myself c'nsid'able beholden to skunks."

"Bah gosh," said Antoine, "Ah don' fred for skonk. me! Ah tek hol' of it hees tails an' lif' 'im aup, he can' do sometings! No, sah!"

"'Twouldn't make no diff'ence tu ye if he did," said Lisha; a skunk's nat-ral weepon hain't nothin' but double d'stilled biled-daown essence of inyuns, 'n' ye couldn't hurt a Canuck wi' that."

"Bah gosh, guess you fin' aout 'f he hurt you, you git him on you heyesight, whedder you Canuck or somebody. Ant it, Peltiet, hein?"

Said Solon Briggs, "Might I arise to ask you, Antwine, Anthony, or Anto-ni-o, all of which I suppose you ter be, haow du you prevent the aout-squirtin' of the viles o' wrath whilst you air a-proachin' of the mestiforious quadruple head?"

"Wal, M'sieu Brigg, dat someting you got t' larn bah —ah—what you call it, pracsit?"

"Perhaps Peltier 'd lend ye one o' his'n to practyse on, Solon," Lisha suggested, but Solon expressed no desire to acquire the art of capturing skunks by that method.

"They raly can't scent when you hol' 'em up by the tail, 'n' that's a fact," said Joseph Hill. "I remember onct when I was a boy ten 'r dozen year ol'—I d'know, mebby I was fourteen—lemme see, 'twas the year 't father hed the brindle caow die 't hed twin calves; got choked with an apple—no 't wa'n't, t'was a tater—they was fo' ye'r oles when he sole 'em, the fall 't I was seventeen—no, I wa'n't but thirteen—the' was a skunk got int' the suller, 'n' of course we didn't want to kill 'im there, so my oldest brother, Lije, he took a holt on 'im by the tail an' kerried 'im aout the hatchway with a pair o' tongs, an' then he gin 'im to me, an' I hel' 'im up while he shot 'im. He put the ol' gun clus to his head an' blowed 'im clean aouten the tongs as fur 's crost this shop, 'n' by gol, he never scent one mite till then, no more 'n' a snowball."

"Did he die?" asked the ever-alert seeker after useful knowledge.

"Why, yes," Joseph replied, "he jes' stunk hisself to death, then."

"Jozeff," said Lisha, "that 'ere puts me in mind of the Paddy. 'Divil a nade o' shootin' him,' says he; 'lave him alone, an' sure he'll shtink himself to death.' What a 'tarnal time the creeturs du hev wi' skunks 'fore they git 'quainted with 'em. 'Member the ol' story one on 'em tol'? What was't, Sam?"

Sam repeated the time honored tale. "'The furs toime iver I wint hoontin' in Ameriky was wan day whin I was gown to me woruk, an' I kilt a boird call't a skoonk. I threed hur undher a hayshtack an' shot hur wid me sphade, an' the furs toime I hit hur I misht hur, an' the nixt toime I hit hur where I misht hur afore. An' whin

I wint to plook the feathers off hur, I was foorced to shkin hur, an' in doun that I shtruck hur ile bag or hur heart I dunno, an' the shmell nearly suffocaytit me, an' I was near shtarvin' afther, for divil a dhrink cud I take, but the shmell of hur was in me noshtrils to kape me awake all night.' I like to died," Sam continued, "to hear Joel Bartlett's Irishmun tell 'baout the fust skunk 't he ever met. 'Twas when he was in Masschusitts, ' Maxacushin ' he called it. He ben a-workin' on a railroad, an' lived in a shanty as yit, though he was workin' fer a farmer. Says he, ' I wor a-shpadin' round threes in a yoong archard, an' Tom Egan, the divil, was in id wid me, an' I seen caperin' troo the grass a foine shlip av a young cat, an' says I to Tom, says I, " Begob, I'll capshure it to kill the mice in the curse o' God shanty that's near dhrivin' me dishthracktit." "Do," says he to me, an' the divil knowin' in his own moind what it was. An' away I wint in purshuit, an' whin I was about to lay me two hands on id, I was shtruck in me face an' the two eyes av me wid a shtream av the divil's own wather, an' I was blindit an' shtrangled entirely. But I joomped on the baste wid me boots an' kilt it, I was that choked wid rage, an' a grea' d'l beside, an' thin I wint away back to Tom, but divil a near him wud he let me come, the bla'gyard, an' I call't out, " Tom !" says I, " am I kilt entirely, an' is it me, or is it the divil's father of a baste that be's makin' the notorious shtink altogether?" says I. " Begob !" says he, " it's the both ov yees, an' ye'll shmell that bad an' maybe worse for a year," says he. " Ah, thin," I cried, " millia murthers, I'm ruinaytit !" an' so skoolked away home to the curse o' God shanty, an' whin I wint in Biddy an' the childher wint out, an' I had the shanty an' the shmell all to meself. Well, I berrit me clo's, an' I sailed back an' forth troo the pond o' wather till night, but divil a much betther did I shmell for a week. Oh, bad luck to the counthry that nurtures such cats!'"

" Dat Arish," Antoine remarked, "a'nt spik so good Angleesh lak Ah do, don't it?"

The slim candle in the sconce had burned so low that when Lisha attempted to snuff it with his fingers he pulled it out and it dropped upon the floor, and sputtering out, left the shop in darkness except for the thin streaks of firelight that shone through the cracks of the stove and the dim rays of stars slanting in at the little window. The mishap was accepted as a unanimous vote of adjournment, and stumbling and groping their way to the door, Lisha's guests again departed.

VI.

HOW ZENE BURNHAM COME IT ON HIS FATHER.

The first snowfall of the season was sifting down on the little valley from a dull sky one November evening when Lisha's friends began to gather in his little shop. Each one, as he entered and stamped the snow off his boots, made some remark concerning this latest turn of the weather, as in duty bound by ancient usage: "Snowin'," "Snowin' c'nsid'able kind o' smart," "Gittin' some snow at last," said one and another, and one ventured to "guess 't we're goin' to git some sleighin' fur Thanksgivin', arter all."

"Wal, I d' know 'baout that," said the oracular Solon Briggs, seating himself in the best place behind the stove, with his elbows on his knees and his hands spread to catch the heat; "I knowed 'at 't was goin' to snow, an' said 't was, an' it does snow, but I took a notice every sen' I commenced my pilligridge (I wou' say, my pilgigrim) that when the snow comes on ter the graound when it's conjoled—that is, when it's froze, it hain't a-goin' t' stay on an' *en*-dure long. Why it is I do' know, but so it is as fur as my observations has went."

"Honh!" snorted Lisha, who was rummaging a shelf for a desired last; "mebby so, but I guess—No. 12, that's it—I guess 't we'll hev sleighin' fur Thanksgivin'. But dum the sleighin', I wish 't I hed a turkey fer Thanksgivin' 's big 's what my boy 't lives in the 'Hio tells o' hevin' there, wild ones, tu, 't weighs thirty, forty paound! What ye think o' that?"

"I daoubt it," was Sam Lovel's laconic response, and there was a stir of approval in the audience.

"Daoubt it!" shouted Lisha. "Good airth an' seas! my boy wouldn't lie an aounce on the weight of a elephant. Thirty 'n' forty paound, that's what he writ."

"Wal, I daoubt it," Sam repeated; "jes' think on 't, that's mos' half as much as Cap'n Power's hawg weighed, 'n' he was a sollaker, ye know. Turkeys ain't in the habit o' growin' so big."

"Not here, I know they hain't," Lisha admitted.

"No," Solon interrupted, "fer it hain't their nart'ral climax. They hain't abregoines here." *

"No," Lisha continued, "'n' then things grows bigger there 'n' what they does here. Why, the corn grows so high 't they have to climb up a ladder to bind the stooks, 'n' my boy writ 't the punkins grow'd so big in the 'Hio that a six-foot man stan'in' stret up couldn't tech the top on 'em! What ye think o' that?"

"Oh, shaw! Git aout! Go to grass!" were the comments on this statement.

"Yes, boys, it's sartinly so," Lisha persisted, with the twinkle of his eyes showing through his dim glasses. "I didn't scacely b'lieve it myself, 'n' I sot down 'n' writ George a letter 'n' ast 'im ef that was r'aly so, an' he writ back it sartinly was. A six-foot man couldn't tech the top o' one on 'em—not 'thaout stoopin' jest a lee-tle. Haw! Haw! Haw! Ho!"

---

* Solon is supposed to have meant aborigines.

"Oh, aw," said Solon. "Yes, George writ ironical, in sportyve jeest, as it ware."

"Wal," said Lisha, when he had done laughing, and had got the last inside of a great boot that needed tapping, "le's p'cede to business, 's they say in the leegislatur. We was talkin' 'baout aowls t' other night, wa'n't we? Solon he tol' what made 'em hoot, 'n' Jozeff he tol' 'baout shootin' one. Hain't ye got nothin' furder concernin' the faowl, Jozeff?"

"I d' know," Joseph Hill responded. "Lemme see. Didn't none on ye never hear how Zene Burnham come it on his father?"

If any one had heard it he made no sign, and Joseph proceeded with his tale.

"Yes, sir, his own father! Oh, what a darned crutter he was! Ye know the' hain't no spring nigh the ole man's, so they've got a well; puty good water, tew—that is, for water, with a reg'lar ole-fashion sweep—do' know though, mebby they've got in a pump naow. Lemme see, didn't Morrison sell 'm a pump? Seem t' me 't he did. Wal, 't do' make no diffunce, they hed a well-sweep then. One night in the fall—I guess 'twas; yes, know 'twas well 'nough, for fall's the aowliest time o' year—Zene he come tippytoein' int' the haouse 'n' spoke low t' the ol' man, an' says he, 'Father, the's the all-tummuttablest gret hoot aowl a-settin' on the top o' the well-sweep! Git the gun an' shoot 'im. You c'n shoot better 'n I can in the dark.' The ol' man kinder thought Zene was a-foolin' on 'im, but Zene said for 'im to go an' see for hisself; so the ole man got the gun, 'n' 'twas loaded for fox, an' stuck a piece o' white paper ont' the sight, an' crep' aout the back door 'n' raound t' the naw-west corner o' the haouse—lemme see ; no, 'twas the naw-east—no twa'n't nuther, 'twas the naw-west corner—an' peeked raound, 'n' there he seen the aowl, an ol' whopper, settin' up there, jes' as demute! An' he drawed up an' took dead aim, he did, 'n' onhitched, 'n' the aowl never stirred! 'Wal, I'll be dummed to dumnation,' says he, ' What 'n thunderation 's the motter I didn't kill 'im? You ben drawin' the shot aouten this gun, Zene?' 'Hain't teched the darned ol' gun,' says Zene. ' You hit 'im in the head an' stunted 'im; load up an' give 'im 'nother dost,' says he. So they went back in an' loaded up agin, an' the ol' man crep' aout agin, 'n' there sot the aowl yit, an' the ol' man blazed away agin, 'n' by gosh! the aowl never stirred agin! Then the ol' man he swore it beat the devil, if 't wa'n't the devil hisself, but Zene tole 'im 't he knowed he'd killed 'im. ' Pull daown the sweep,' says he, ' 'n' git 'im. He's sartinly deader 'n hay.' So the ol' man sot daown the gun an' begin tu pull daown the sweep jes' as keerful, a-watchin' the aowl all the time as he come daown, never makin' a motion. When he git him clus tu an' was jest a-goin' to take a holt on 'im, he seen 't wa'n't nothin' but a all-fired gret big cabbage tied on t' the end of the sweep! My! 'f the ol' man wa'n't mad! Zene he put er for in t' the haouse 'n' upstairs 'n' int' bed, 'n' by mornin' the ol' man hed got good natur'd agin, but ye didn't want to say ' aowl ' to him right off.''

"Did he hit the cabbage?" was asked by him of an inquiring turn of mind.

"Those 'ere saw-whet aowls," Solon Briggs remarked, clearing his throat, " is a curosity thing—a frik o' natur' comin' daown to her onsignificantest teches—a nart'ral fewnonnymon, so to speak. A puffick aowl, minus the gretness of the die-mentionist kinds."

"Wal, they be small, but reg'lar aowls," said Sam Lovel. "Cut the head off 'm one 'n' he'll lack a aounce o' weighin'. I shot one on 'em outen a tree jes' to see what he was, 'n' he come a-floatin' daown julluk a bunch o' feathers."

"An' their vocal voice," put in Solon, "is the fact smile of sharpnin' a saw."

"Guess 't is," said Sam, "egg-zack! Makes me think o' one time t' ol' Mist' Van Brunt f'm New York 's up here a-lookin' arter his lumbrin' intrus. 'Twas long airly 'n the spring 'n' he was ridin' 'long hoss-back 'n the evenin', 'n' when he got daown int' Stunny Brook holler, he hearn someb'dy a-filin' a sawmill saw, *screet er screet, er screet er*. 'Some o' them dum maounting Aribs,' says he, 'hes got a sawmill right here in the hairt o' my woods! Hello you!' he hollered, but the file kep' a-goin', *screet er screet, er screet!* 'You owdacious villing!' says he—he allus used high duck langwuage— 'you owdacious villing! I'll prosecute ye to the extents o' the law,' says he, and he rid his hoss int' the woods where he hearn the noise, 'n' his sto'pipe hat ketched on a limb an' tumbled off, 'n' his hoss stumbled agin a ruht 'n' throwed 'im off, 'n' then the noise o' filin' stopped, 'n' then in two, three minutes it begin agin furder off. 'The pirutical scoundril,' says the ol' gentleman, 'hez got his dum sawmill on wheels!' 'n' he got back int' the path an' rid ont' the tarvern 'thaout no hat. When he got there he tol' Hamlin (he kep' it then) what he'd hearn, 'n' Hamlin he laughed, 'n' says he, 'Mist' Van Brunt, 't wa'n't nothin' but a saw-whet 't you hearn.' 'A saw-whet!' says th' ol' gentleman, 'I know it, but a two-legged saw-whet, sir.' 'Yes,' says Hamlin, ' two-legged, but he wears feathers stiddy clo's,' 'n' 'xplained. Then the ol' gentleman laughed at hisself, an' treated the hull craowd, a dozen on 'em, to ole Jamaiky sperrits 't he brought with him f'm York—twenty ye'r ole, they said 't was."

"Gosh!" ejaculated Joseph Hill, with a watering mouth, " wish 't I'd a ben there!"

" Ben where?" asked he of the inquiring mind.

" The study of nart'ral hist'ry things," Solon remarked, " is a most stumenduous subjeck, cal'lated to fill the human mind of man with—er—er—ah—"

" Puddin' an' milk," shouted Lisha, as he drove the last peg in the wide sole of the boot, " 'n' I 'tend to ha' some an' go to bed."

So saying he took off his battle-scarred apron, and his guests departed, and faded with silent footsteps into the dusky whiteness of the snowy night.

VII.

A RAINY DAY IN THE SHOP.

ONE gloomy day in November several of Uncle Lisha's friends, realizing the fact that it rained too hard to "work aou' door," that it was too wet even for comfortable hunting, and that it was too late in the season for fishing, betook themselves singly and in couples to the shop to pass away the time which hung with unendurable heaviness upon their hands at home. There was a genial warmth radiating from the full fed rusty little stove, and a mild sunshine from the kindly face of the old shoemaker that made the rude interior seem exceedingly comfortable in contrast with the dismal chill and dampness of the outdoor world, and the clatter of the hammer on the lapstone was a much more cheerful sound than the leaden patter of the rain on roof and pane and fallen leaves. But though tne new-comers gave some impassive signs of appreciation of the change from out-door discomfort to in-door comfort, they seemed to have brought in with them too much of the exterior atmosphere ; it exhaled from their wet garments and dulled spirits till their host felt it and resented it.

"Good airth an' seas, boys, what's the motter ails ye, all on ye? Ye ain't no sociabler 'n a passel o' snails holdin' a meetin' 'n under a cabbage leaf! 'Tain't a fun'el. By mighty, it's wus, for the' hain't no preachin' ner singin', ner even sighthin' ner cryin'. Why don't some on ye up an' die an' kinder liven up things a leetle mite, hey?"

While Solon Briggs was swelling up with explanatory words too big for speedy utterance, Joseph Hill remarked, as he searched all his pockets for the pipe and tobacco that he never knew where to find, "I 'spect, as Joel Bartlett says when he takes a notion to start off on a preachin' taower, 'at we've all on us got a weighty consarn on aour mind, Uncle Lisher."

"Wal, Jozeff hes spoke, an' that's incouragin'. Naow, let another, as Brother Foot says in prayer-meetin'."

"Jozeff's speakin'," continued Uncle Lisha, after waiting a moment for a response, " puts me in mind o' his dawg 'at he uster hev, 'at nob'dy never knowed to du nothin' on'y eat an' sleep, an' bark a' folks goin' 'long 'baout the' business, an' at the moon nights, when folks was extry tired an' wantin' t' sleep more 'n common but couldn't, 'caount o' his 'tarnal bow-wowin' an' yollopin'. Jozeff, howsever, was allus a-tellin' what a good dawg he was, an' even went the len'th o' sayin' 't he was harnsome! A yaller dawg, an' harnsome! Hain't that so, Jozeff? Don't ye deny it!" he roared, glaring at his visitor between his eyebrows and the rims of his spectacles, as he began to fashion a slow, dubious " wal " with his lips. "Yes," he continued, " good an' harnsome, he said he was. You never seen a man 'at hed him a dawg 'at wa'n't a-braggin' 'baout him on some pint. That's one reason 'at I don't hev me a dawg. I hain't no gift o' braggin'. 'Nuther is, I hain't no use for a dawg in my business. Wal," picking out the soggy " heel " of his pipe with a crooked awl, " one day when Samwill here an' 'mongst 'em was exhaltin' of the' horns an' a-blowin' on 'em 'baout the' haoun' dawgs, Jozeff he up an' begin blowin' his'n abaout his'n. Someb'dy nuther ast him, 'What'll he du? Did he ever tree a coon?' 'No,' says Jozeff. 'Er hole a woo'chuck?' 'No.' 'Er drive a k'yow er a hawg?' 'Wal, not ezackly drive 'em.' 'Er ta' keer o' the haouse?' 'Wal, he's allus there, but I do' know 's he raly takes keer on't.' 'Wal, then, what on airth is he good for?' 'Wal,' says Jozeff, says he, arter c'nsid'able c'nsid'rin', 'he's comp'ny!' An'," said Uncle Lisha when he had blown through his pipe after clearing the stem with a waxed end, "I'll be dum'd 'f I wouldn't druther hev Jozeff Hill's ol' yaller dawg for comp'ny 'n t' hev sech a consarned mumpin' set as you be."

The only responses were a general though feeble and perfunctory laugh and an apologetic remark from Solon Briggs that "when the caloric of the warmth had penetrated the water aouten their garments they would be more conversationabler," which Antoine endeavored to make more easily comprehended by explaining, "Yas, Onc' Lasha, when we'll gat aour froze t'aw aout we'll got aour speak t'aw aout."

A little later the constant searcher for information broke the silence by asking Joseph Hill, "Whatever be become o' that 'ere dawg 'at Uncle Lisher ben speakin' on?"

"M'ri sol' him tu a peddler," said Joseph, with a sigh of regret for his lost companion. "M'ri didn't never set no gret store by dawgs, though the' be women 'at likes to hev a dawg 'raound, for all the' makin' b'lieve hate 'em —likes to hev 'em 'raound to lay things onter, bad smells an' sech, an' broken airthenware, an' t' 'buse—wal, I do' know as 'buse ezackly, but tu vent the' feelin's on. But

M'ri never 'bused Liern, though I don't think he raly 'nj'yed her comp'ny, 'specially moppin' days an' when she was sweepin' aout."

" Wal, I do' know's I blame anybody much for mumpin' sech weather," said Uncle Lisha, relenting, as while he ground the pegs from the inside of a newly-tapped boot he gazed abstractedly out of the rain-pelted little window upon the blurred landscape ; the sodden dun fields bounded by the gray wall of mountain with its drifting coping of mist—all dun and gray but for one poplar that shone like a pale flame among the ashy trunks and branches of its burned-out companions, and when a gust fanned it, showered down its yellow leaves like sparks from a flaring torch. " I do' know 's I blame any on ye much ; sech weather 's turrible hefty on the sperits. 'F I hed me a pint, er mebby a quart o' cider brandy, er ol' Jamacky sperits, I raly b'lieve I'd git so condemned boozy 't I couldn't see aouten the winder—'f 't wa'n't for makin' an' mendin' these 'ere dum'd ol' boots an' shoes, I would, by golly blue !"

" I snum ! I sh'ld like ter help ye, Uncle Lisher," said Joseph Hill, smacking his lips.

" 'N' it's mos' Thanksgivin' time," Lisha went on ; " I b'lieve the day's ben sot by the Gov'ner, hain't it ? Seem's 'ough I seen it in the last *V'monter*. Jerushy !" He called so loudly and suddenly that it startled all his guests, and again " Jerushy !" with a roar that made the battered stove-pipe jingle. " Be you deaf or be you dead ?"

" What—on—airth ?" asked the mildly astonished old matron as she opened the door just wide enough to let her nose and voice into the shop.

"Gim me that 'ere last paper; I wanter see 'f Thanksgivin' Day 's 'pinted. It's eyther in the stan' draw, erless in the cub'd, 'f ye hain't got some o' yer everlastin' yarbs spread onter it in the chahmber."

"Yarbs!" Aunt Jerusha replied from the "house part," where she could be heard wrestling with the refractory stand drawer, and then rummaging among papers, "why, good land o' Goshen, Lisher, my yarbs was all dried an' in the' bags 'fore ever that 'ere paper thought o' bein' printed! Naow, seem 's 'ough you took it to wrap up Miss Bartlett's bootees in t'other day. Oh, no, here 't is"—reappearing in the doorway—"I b'lieve, le' me see," "tromboning" the paper to get the proper focus of her glasses, "October the thirty—yes; here, Lisher," groping her way to her lord through the tobacco smoke and rubbish and legs of visitors, and then as through the reek she began to recognize one and another—"Oh, hope I see ye well, Mr. Briggs an' Mr. Hill. Miss Briggs an' Miss Hill, be they well? Turrible spell o' weather we're a-hevin' on. Why, haow du you du, Samwill? Be you well, Antwine? an' haow's your womern? My! haow you men du smoke! I can't scasely see who's who. Wal, I s'pose terbarker is comfortin' sech weather for them 'at c'n stan' it, but I never could," and she retreated, tapping her snuff-box as she went.

"As if snuff wa'n't terbarker!" Uncle Lisha snorted after her. "Le's see," spreading the paper on his knees and staring at it naked-eyed while he wiped his glasses on his shirt sleeve; then, adjusting them astride his nose with unusual care. "Le' me see—'Scott an' Raymon' offer —m—m—'Partrick Foster, groceries an' p'visions' (an' hoss rum) m—m—m—'B. Seym'r, hats an' caps an' highest price fer fur'—oh, here 't is—' Proclermatiern by the Gov'ner—'Cordin' to suthin' nuther usage 'n' so f'th, 'n' so f'th, hm—m—m—I du hereby 'pint Thursd'y the twenty-sev'mph day o' November as a day o' thanksgivin'.' Wonder what they allus hev it come a Thursd'y for, and Fast Day Frid'y? Dum'd 'f I know. An' 'lection day an' taown meetin' an' the leegislatur' begin settin' a Tuesd'y. Mebby that's so 's 't the men c'n hev clean shirts on ; though the' hain't time for i'nin on 'em—more likely it's cause the men folks is fresh f'm the disciplyne o' washin' day, an' more cal'lated to du the' duty. Hm! so Thanksgivin' comes tew weeks f'm nex' Thursd'y, hey? What be I goin' t' du f'r a turkey, I sh' like t' know? We hain't raised none, an' I can't 'ford to buy one, an' I've got tu ol' an' dim-sighted t' shoot one tu a-shootin' match—do' know 's the' 's goin' t' be one, anyway."

"Yas," some one said, "Hamner 's layin' 'aout t' hev a turkey shoot, Thanksgivin'."

"Ya-us," Joseph Hill contemptuously assented, "he's a-cal'latin' tu hev what might posserbly be called a turkey shoot. He's got him fifteen er twenty leetle teenty tawnty faowls 't he calls turkeys—hatched in August, do' know 's they was fore September, nary one on 'em bigger 'n a cardy bird *—do' know but they be bigger 'n cardy birds, but pleggid little to speak on, an' he'll set 'em up forty rod, I do' know but fifty, at a York shillin' a shot! The' hain't nob'dy, erless it's Sam here, c'ld hit one shootin' a week that fur off. 'N' one on 'em would n't more 'n go 'raound 'mong tew hearty folks—do' know 's the' 'ld be 'nough for tew. He hedn't ort to set 'em up not to say more 'n fifteen er twenty rod, ner ast over 'n'

---

* Nuthatch.

above fo'p'nce ha'p'ny a shot, at sech leetle teenty tawnty insi'nificant creeturs, an' then he'd make money aout on 'em."

"Hamner is tew narrer-c'ntracted an' peniverous tu be very satisfactual tu his patrings," Solon Briggs remarked. "He is a very parsinumerous man."

"Did ye notice haow Solon's bloat went daown," Joseph whispered huskily, nudging with his elbow the ribs of his neighbor on the seat behind the stove, "when he got them big words aouten on him?" He'll hev one on 'em in him some day 'at'll swell up an' bust him 'fore he gits red on't, see 'f he don't. Do' know 's it'll bust him, but it'll strain his riggin' turribly—yes," he said aloud, in confirmation of Solon's opinion of the unpopular landlord, "he's all o' them. They du say as he waters his ol' Medford rum 'at costs him thirty cents a gallern, an' him a-sellin' on't at fo'pence ha'p'ny a glass. Anyways, it's dreffle weak. A man 'ould git draounded in't 'fore he'd git tu feelin' good on't. I guess he would putty nigh."

"Good airth an' seas! I don't b'lieve the critter keeps nothin' but hoss rum. Tew drinks on't clear 'ould knock a feller higher 'n Gilderoy's kite, so it's a massy to them 'at drinks it 'at he does thin it wi' water," said Uncle Lisha, as he generously daubed the edges of the tap with lampblack and oil. "I tell ye what you du, Samwill. You gwup to Hamner's turkey shoot an' git me a turkey—git tew 'f ye'r a minter, an' come t' aour Thanksgivin'. The' 'll be a turkey for me an' Jerushy, an' one for you—one for us tew an' one for you tew, 's the Irishmun said when he was dividin' the four dollars 'twixt himself an' his tew frinds. Er she c'n hev the necks o' both—she's allus a-tellin' haow the necks is the bes' part of a faowl, an' you 'n' I'll take the stuffin' an' what's left. I'll pay for tew shots an' you pay for tew, an' 'f you can't git tew turkeys aout o' four shots you hain't the man 't I take ye t' be. What d' yo' say, Samwill?"

"I'd a good deal druther git ye some patridges, Uncle Lisher. Dum this blazin' away at a poor mis'able turkey sot top of a barrel with his laigs tied, scairt half to death with the balls zippin' raound him. 'Tain't no fun for me. I'd druther go out in the woods an' git ye tew three patridges."

"Well, patridges then," said the shoemaker; "I don't keer, on'y patridges ain't ezackly sech reg'lar Thanksgivin' meat as turkeys is."

"But the' 's more meat in one good Tom patridge 'an the' is in the hull flock o' Hamner's turkeys," said Joseph Hill. Then, after a little consideration of this statement, "Wal, I do' know 's the hull on 'em, but half on 'em, say."

"Wal, then, call it patridges," said Uncle Lisha, with a sigh of resignation. "We'll go it on punkin pie an' patridges. Will ye git 'em, Samwill?"

"You sh'll hev 'em, Uncle Lisher," Sam said, sitting upright from leaning against the wall, his promise emphasized by the creak of the roll of sole leather he sat upon, "'f the's any in the woods."

"Oh, the woods is popular with 'em," said Solon. "I scairt one aouten my woodshed yist'd'y mornin', er mebby 'twas day 'fore yist'd'y mornin'—any ways, I scairt one aout on't when I went aout arter kin'lin', an' I tol' M'ri on't."

"Proberly the's so much wood in your shed, Jozeff, 'at he thought he was in the woods," said Uncle Lisha, whittling a plug of tobacco on his cutting-board.

"Bah gosh!" cried Antoine, who had long suffered with silence, "'f dey don't tick in de hwood! an' he don't 'fraid more as hen was. Bah gosh! 'todder day, seh, when Ah'll was be choppin' in de hwood dey was one of it flewed raght in ma face, an' Ah'll bite hees head wid ma mouf! Ah'll peek ma toof more as two nour fore Ah'll got de fedder off of it. Bah gosh! Ah'll got a!' de patridge Ah'll wan' for heat more as dis year, dat tam, me."

"Git Antwine to set his maouth an' ketch ye some," Joseph suggested.

"He'd pizon 'em with his dum peasoup lies," growled Uncle Lisha, as he brushed the tobacco into his hand and began grinding it between his palms. "Say, Samwill, haow was you a-cal'latin' to spend yer Thanksgivin' this year? Naow, 'f yer goin' huntin' for me, I want ye t' 'tend right tu yer huntin' an' nothin' else."

There was a roguish twinkle in the corner of the eye nearest the reclining hunter as the old man asked, "Boys, I do' know's I ever tol' ye 'baout this 'ere gret hunter's a-goin' foxhuntin' one Thanksgivin' Day back o' Pur'n't'n's, did I?"

"Uncle Lisher," Sam drawled in a slow, impressive monotone, "if you raly want me tu git you some patridges for Thanksgivin', you don't wanter tell no stories baout my Thanksgivin's."

"You mean it, Samwill?" Lisha asked, pausing in the lighting of his pipe till the match began to fry the wax on his thumb.

"Sartinly I du," Sam answered.

"Wal, then," said Lisha, "I want them patridges, an' I got t' hev 'em," and though Antoine cried, "Tol' it, Onc' Lasha, tol' it! What you cared? Bah gosh! Ah'll know where dat turkey Hamny's roos', an' 'f Ah don't gat you more turkey as you'll heat an' A'n' Jerrushy in four day, Ah'll give you masef for roas' ! Ah'll bet you head, boy, dat Sam shoot fox an' he'll ant hit heem !" and though all beset him importunately, the old man utterly refused to tell the story, and presently his visitors departed in as bad humor as they had come. As they separated at the door yard gate to go their several ways, the inquirer turned back to ask, " Say, Jozeff, haow much did M'rier git for that 'ere dawg ?"

VIII.

THE TURKEY SHOOT AT HAMNER'S.

The morning of the day before Thanksgiving was bright and still, promising such a day as a rifleman would wish for target-shooting, and before the middle of the forenoon almost every man in Danvis who owned a rifle, and some who did not, but were enough in favor to borrow one of owners too old to use one, or too impecunious to share in a sport that called for a "York shillin'" a shot, was at Hamner's hostelry, or hurrying toward it across lots or along the rough, frozen roads. And as many or more than these were those who went with hands in pockets, otherwise empty, to look on enviously, and rugged-faced old mountaineers whose dim eyes could no longer sight a rifle, and whose palsied hands had shaken off all their cunning, to criticise the younger shooters and tell marvellous tales of what they could do and had done in bygone years; and also penniless and stingy topers who scented occasional free drinks among the possibilities of the meeting. One of them, standing in the middle of the road, slowly spelled out the words on the sign which the proprietor had lately hung out under the eaves of the smart and flimsy new piazza, "H, a, m, Ham, n, e, r, s, ner's, h, o, t, hot, e, l, le, hottle! Humph! I wonder if the rum-m-m [his lips clung fondly to this comprehensive name for all alcoholic intoxicants] in a hottle is any better 'n what it uster be in a tarvern? I'd a darn sight druther see the ol' sign stuck up on the post aout there, 'Tarvern—cnt'tainmint for man an' beast.'"

"Wal, it sartingly did look more horsepitiful," said Solon Briggs, turning his critical glance from the new sign to the old post still standing, though uncrowned, by the roadside. "But this is a age of reprovement, 'Niram, an' ol' things is dis-pearin' an' new things is a-pearin'."

"Say, 'Niram," cried the most smartly dressed young fellow in the crowd on the piazza, "du you ever drink anything naow-er-days?"

"Wal, I du," thirsty Adoniram promptly responded, "when I can't git snow t' eat!" and casting out his quid he bent his steps in the direction of the prospective treat, following close at the heels of the young man as he led the way into the bar-room. When Adoniram had poured his gill of raw spirits down his throat, his entertainer called his attention to a showily-trimmed rifle standing within the safe precincts of the bar. "There, 'Niram, is what you may call a linger gun. Reach it aout here, Hamner. That's the weepon 'at's agoin' t' pop the turkeys to-day! Haint it a steeple-picker?" brushing its German silver ornaments with his coat-sleeve and sighting one of the tack-heads which held a horse advertisement to the wall. "Thirty-five dollars in money I paid Varney for makin' on it, an' he warr'nts it t' fetch 'em every time! The' haint nob'dy livin', you know, 'at c'n beat Varney— Burl'nt'n, you know—a makin' a rifle. Naow, look a here," seating himself on the bunk, which was the principal article of furniture in the room, and motioning Adoniram to a place beside him, and lowering his voice to a privately confidential mumble, "when they git a turkey sot up, an' I'm a goin' tu hev a shot, I want you, 'Niram, tu kinder gwup half way er so, an' kinder drop yer hat off, sorter accident'l, so 's 't I c'n see haow much wind the' is a stirrin' aout there. 'F you'll be clever 'nough t' du that much for me, 'Niram, you sha'n't suffer none f'm bein' dry t'day!"

"I will du it, *Mi*ster Putman!" said Adoniram, emphasizing his promise with a stroke of his fist upon his knee, " not 'at I keer a darn for hevin' a drink er tew gi'n me, but aouten clear frien'ship! Me an' yer father was allus frien's, went t' school tugether, 'n' got lickin's, 'n' fit, 'n' eat one other's nutcakes, 'n' everything, an' I'm a goin' t' du his son a good turn whence ever I git a chance, I be! Yes, *sir!* Ahem! Seems 's 'ough that 'ere spoo'f'l o' rum was a feelin' kinder lunsome in my in'ards, *Mi*ster Putman."

"Ex-cuse me, 'Niram, I was jest a-goin' to ask ye 'f you wa'n't a gettin' dry. Set aout yer best, Hamner; 'taint none tu good for my frien's."

"Hamner's rum an' the river is putty clust neighbors," Adoniram remarked, remembering to smack his lips only when the last drop of his generous potation had passed them. " This 'ere don't seem to take a holt much."

"That's the clear quill, 'Niram," said the publican, pouring a spoonful into a glass and smelling and tasting it. "The clear quill, fourth proof, cost me — le' me see—"

"Clear quill!" Adoniram broke in on his calculations, "duck quills an' geese quills, I guess like 's not. They was a tellin'," bestowing impartial winks on the son of his friend and the proprietor of the hotel, " haow someb'dy 'nuther faound a minny alive an' kickin' in his sperits here t'other day!"

"Hello, Jeems! Hello, 'Nirum! well-named, wa'n't ye? Allus nigh rum when it's araound!" cried a big, bluff new-comer with a heavy rifle lying as lightly as a reed in the hollow of his arm. "Come, Hamner, set up them 'ere poultry an' le's hev a crack at 'em!"

"Wal, it is about time we was at it," young Putnam assented, hauling out a gold-plated watch and consulting it ostentatiously, "seven minutes t' ten!"

"Sartinly, sartinly, Mr. Dart; I was only a-waitin' for the folks tu rest 'em an' stiddy the narves an' re-fresh 'emselves up. You're a lee-tle faster 'n what I be, Mr. Putnam," said Hamner, looking at the bar-room clock.

"I sot my watch by Austin's t' V'gennes last week, an' he reg-lates the sun," Putnam asserted.

"Pshaw! Hamner," said Dart, after looking at the tall clock and listening attentively a moment, "yer pleggid ol' m'chine 's stopped runnin'! You'd orter hev a crank stuck int' yer ol' minute-mill an' take a day an' grind aout time anough t' last ye a week! But I see yer idee. You wanter git us so 's 't we can't see a hole through a ladder 'fore you let us shoot! Wal, le' me 'speriment wi' yer pison. I'll resk one drink. Come, Jeems an' 'Nirum, le's die together. Here 's a hopesin' 'at we'll pass away kinder comf'table. There, Hamner, 's a nimep'nce, an' that 'ill pay for aour drinks, bein' 't we're all light drinkers, 'specially 'Nirum. Naow, Hamner, you take it an' don't ye grumble. You c'n buy a pint o' proof sperits wi' nimep'nce, 'n' that'll make a gallern o' sech nourishment 's this. Say, boys, hev another an' I'll give him a quarter. Little haint much, an' twicte haint often! No? Wal, then, le's go 'n' kill one of Hamner's chickadees 'fore we die."

The outbuildings of the tavern straggled along the bank of the intervale, on the broadest part of which was room enough—too much, some thought—for the range. Beyond the stable was the stand, which was simply a plank with one end resting on a horse, the other on the ground, and out toward the furthest curve of the little river stood a dry-goods box on which the turkeys were to be placed. "Thunder in the winter!" Dart ejaculated, as he looked over the range with a half-shut, calculating eye, "you call that forty rod, Hamner? M'asured it with an injin-rubber string, didn't ye, 'n' pulled like a yoke o' stags? I sh' like t' buy the interv'l 'cordin' to that m'asure. But set one up!"

The long, lank, sharp-faced publican directed an assistant to bring out a turkey, and after a fluttering commotion in the stable he reappeared with a half-grown one under his arm, and took his way across the flat toward the dry-goods box. "Oh, what a turkey!" Dart shouted. "Haint ye got no aigs ter set up? Wal, Hamner, you be tough—tougher 'n a biled aowl! But nev' mind, I'm a goin' ter shoot—that's what I come here for. But a feller might jes' 's well shoot at the moon—'t ain't much furder off, an' it's bigger."

"Wal, yes, some bigger, John," said Joseph Hill, taking off his hat and scratching his head meditatively, "leastways when it's full, which it don't seem as 'ough that turkey was."

"Oh, you shet up, Joe Hill!" Hamner snarled. "Turkeys is what's called for, an' that 'ere 's a turkey, haint it?" and he glowered a sidelong glance at the giant Dart, who, good-natured as he was, looked too big to quarrel with.

"Sartinly, Mr. Hamner," said the amicable Joseph, "that's the name on 't, I haint no daoubt. A turkey 's a turkey soon 's he's hatched."

"Say, Bill!" Dart shouted after the bearer of the turkey, "got any lunchern in yer pocket? You'll git hungry 'fore you git there. An' say, Bill, holler when ye git yer gobbler sot up, so 's 't we'll know. He's most aout o' sight naow!"

At last the poor bird was placed in position, Bill retreated to a safe distance and the cover of the river-bank, and Dart, lying down on the plank, rested his rifle across the end of it. After much sighting and squinting he cocked his piece and, taking careful aim, fired.

"Sol', for a nimep'nce!" he proclaimed, as the turkey was seen to flutter and fall prone upon the box.

"Don't b'lieve ye teched him! He's only scairt!" Hamner snarled, unwilling to believe that his turkey had gone for so little money. But all doubt on that score was removed when Bill took it down and began his journey toward them, a dozen of the party running out to meet him.

"'T won't take more 'n half on ye tu bring in that turkey," Dart called after them. "Naow, Hamner, you be ketchin' another tu set up. I want a mess while I'm 'baout it an' got my hand in."

"Not by a gol darned sight you don't hev another shot! You s'pose I'm a goin' tu hev the bread took aouter my maouth that way? One turkey 's 'nough for anybody but a darned hawg!"

"You're jest right, Hamner. One turkey 's as much as anybody 'd ort tu eat tu oncte, an' all I want is one apiece for the fam'ly. The' 's five on us, none on us very hearty t' eat only gran'maw 'n' the baby, an' five turkeys is all 't I want. But the' haint nothin' small 'baout me only my feet," holding out a No. 12 " stogy" for inspection, " which you may not think they be, but a feller's boot haint his foot. Mine 's small, but a big boot fits 'em best. I don't push for the nex' shot. Here's Mr. Putman, which he's got him a rifle 'at cost him thir ty-five dollars in money, an' Varney made it, which that means all you've got t' du is tu show it a turkey an' it fetches him ! An' Mr. Putman wants a few. 'N' here's Peltier Gove, he's got the Widder Wiggins's rifle, which it was Pete's, an' he give Hatch the price of a ye'rlin' colt for it, an' the' 's some 'at says haow Hatch c'n make jes' as good a gun as Varney any day, an' Peltier wants tu find aout. An' here is Jozeff Hill ; he's a luggin' 'raound one o' Seaver's ol' fewzees which they say he *hes* hit a barn with it, bein' 'at he was on the inside on 't an' all the doors shet. An' the' 's lots more on 'em 'at hes tu heng on t' the' guns tu keep 'em f'm goin' off arter turkeys. I'm willin' for half on 'em tu hev a chance while I rest my gun a spell, for it's turrible strainin' on a gun t' shoot so fur. Wal, here's Bill mos' tuckered aout a luggin' of that turkey aout there 'n' back 'thaout restin' much 'n' nothin' t' eat all the time. Le' me see where I hit him. Right in the butt o' the wing ! That's where I allus hit 'em—when I don't miss on 't. Haint he an ol' sollaker ! Sary Ann 'll hefter put the stuffin' on the aoutside—the' haint room 'nough on the inside."

Presently Bill went out with another turkey across the flat, the light snowy covering of which began to show a dun path in the direction of the target. Following him went 'Niram with unsteady footsteps till he got half way across the range, where he halted and threw up his hat with a lusty, if obsolete, cheer for " Tippycanew an' Tyler tew!" As the hat dropped beside him, hardly slanting to the light breeze in its fall, in the exuberance of his spirits, he kicked at it, and missed it, and too topheavy to balance himself, found himself suddenly seated by it. Regarding it for a little with tipsy solemnity, as if wondering " how came we here?" he picked it up, knocked the snow off it, set it upon his head, slowly got himself upon his feet, and meandered back to the stand. The turkey was in position, and the foppishly-dressed young man of the name of Putnam got himself upon the plank with a great flourish of preparation.

"Naow, Jeems," Dart advised as he was sighting his rifle, "you'd better le' me onbutton the strops o' yer trousers, erless you'll pull the tricker off 'm that thirty-five-dollar gun o' yourn er bust yer strops!" But Putnam fired without taking this precaution, and the trigger and straps came safely out of the ordeal, and so did the turkey.

"You 'd orter pulled harder, strops er no strops, an' kinder pushed tew, mebby; a bullit needs helpin' sech long shots. I gi'n mine a boost, 'baout ninety weight, nigh 's I c'ld cal'late."

" This 'ere John Dart a-pears tu be a very jokus individdywil," said Solon Briggs to Joseph Hill; " we hed ort tu give him a invite tu jine aour sore-eyes up tu Lisher's; he would make 'em more convivualler." Joseph hardly understood him, but recommended an alum curd poultice as the best remedy for sore eyes, " thaout 't was lobele steeped intu sperits."

" These 'ere half-len'th rifles hain't wuth a soo markee fer long shots!" Gran'ther Hill whistled savagely, though toothlessly, casting a scornful glance at the thirty-five-dollar rifle and its owner. "I wish 't I hed me my gun here, 'at I hed tu Hubbar't'n an' Bennin't'n, I'd show ye! An' I would ha' hed it 'f I'd hed me a flint 'at hed any more fire in 't 'n a hunk o' col' johnny-cake. Couldn't find nothin' in the haouse but a Injin arrer. Ye can't git a decent flint naow-er-days sen these pesky cap-locks come in fashi'n. Flints is the thing tu tech off paowder, I tell ye! They burns it slow, an' yer ball don't git started fer t' go ontwell the paowder 's all afire, an' then, sir, it goes tu kill! Fo' foot in the berril that 'ere gun is, an' when it's pinted at a thing, you knows it, an' so does what it's pinted at!"

"It ort tu, 'f 'tain't tew fur off," Dart said too loudly.

"Fo' foot in the berril!" the veteran repeated, taking no notice of the interruption but to frown on the speaker, "an' it hain't a inch tew long! Ethin Allin hes shot it, an' so hes Seth Warner, an' so hes Remember Baker, an' so hes John Stark! An' the' don't nobody 'at's here a-shootin' popguns tu-day 'at wants ter up an' tell me 'at they wa'n't shooters an' men 'at knowed what guns was! John Stark says he tu Bennin't'n, says he, 'Them red cuts is aourn, boys, er Molly Stark's a widder! Come on, Josier!' An' tu Hubbar't'n, Seth Warner says he tu me, says he, 'Josier, I want ye tu pick off that 'ere British offycer wi' that long gun o' yourn.' An' sir, a minute arterward that offycer was scase! I was in the fust bwut 'at went aouten Hand's Cove on the tenth o' May, in the mornin' airly, seventeen hund'ed an' seventy-five, an' Ethin Allin was a-standin' in the bow, an' he wa'n't a mite afeared, 'cause I was a settin' right behind of him. Bennydick Arnil was along, tew, the damned traiter, an' I wish 't I hed a-done what I wanted tu, chucked the cussed hook-nosed hen-hawk int' the lake, blast him ! Wal, sir, when we landed an' was drawed up inter line, an' stood a-waitin' an' a-waitin' for the rest on 'em tu come over, Seth an' mongst 'em, an' it begin tu grow light in the East, an' a rwuster begin to crow up tu the fort, Ethin he begin tu git turrible oneasy, an' at last says he, ' If we wait for the rest on 'em any longer, daylight 'll spile aour plan. Every man 'at's willin' tu go for'ad naow, pise his firelock !' An', sir, every man jack on us did it, quicker 'n ever hell scorched a feather ! Then says Ethin, says he, ' Is Josier Hill here ?' ' I be,' says I. ' All right,' says he, ' for'ad, march !' 'Fore we got tu the gate, the' was some squab-blin' 'twixt Ethin an' Arnil 'baout which was a-goin' in fust, an' Ethin come putty nigh a-jabbin' Arnil with his sword ; but they finally fixed it up an' went in 'long side o' one nuther, though I b'lieve I was a leetle mite ahead on 'em, a chasin' the sent'nil 'at snapped at Ethin."

"Golly blue ! Father 'll be a-takin' Canady 'f he gits another underjawful o' Hamner's fightin' rum !" said the veteran's son in mild alarm, and such an exploit seemed not unlikely to be undertaken by the ancient warrior, for he now began to sing in a voice half croak and half whistle, to a small but appreciative audience :

"'We're a-marchin' on tow-wards Quebec,
   Whilst the drums is loudli bea—tin,
   For Americay hes gained the day
   An' the British is retrea—tin' ! '"

"Bah gosh ! Ah'll goin' help it !" cried Antoine, who had been prancing from group to group in search of listeners to what he had to tell concerning shooting. "Dat mek me rembler one tam dey have it shoot-turkey in Canady, an' dey'll ant let you see dem turkey, bah gosh, no! Dey'll have it 'hind a hill of it, an' you'll gat for guess where he'll was an' den shoot. Yes, sah! Well, boy, Ah'll was be dere, an' Ah'll se' dawn an' listen for hear, an' bombye pooty soon Ah'll hear dat turkey beegin for gobbler. Houkle, houkle, houkle! Den Ah'll pant up ma gun up so Ah'll tink de ball was drop off where he'll hit dat nowse, an' Ah'll shot off, pluck! 'Squowk!' Ah'll hear dat turkey said, an' bah gosh! You'll ant b'lieved me, dat ball stroke it raght bit tween hees backs!"

"Oh, beeswax!" said Dart; "they never hed no turkey shoot in Canady! They uster shoot peas at a kittle, an' the one 'at got the most peas into 't 'ould hev the pot o' pea soup made aouten on 'em!"

"Bah gosh, you'll ant know! You'll never was be dere. You'll gat so far from Danvis you'll can' smell spruce gum, you'll ant never fan your way back! Hein! boy?" Antoine retorted.

Putnam made several ineffectual shots, with each his pride in his gun and his faith in its maker falling and failing. Then Pelatiah tried his luck with the work of the rival maker, but its famed killing qualities seemed to have departed with its deceased late owner, much to the sorrow of poor Pelatiah, whose slender weasel skin held but one half dollar, the proceeds of his fall trapping in the Beaver Meadow Brook, and two more shots would exhaust his scant hoard.

Meanwhile Sam Lovel was out in the woods, where he had been long before the shooting began, in pursuit of Uncle Lisha's promised partridges. The frozen leaves, showing a crinkle of brown and here and there a streak or patch of yet unfaded October red and yellow through the light powdering of snow, were noisy under the lightest tread. The squirrels scampering over them in quest of their Thanksgiving fare, could be heard thirty rods away, and a dozen partridges went whirring and crashing away unseen through the haze of gray branches and dark clouds of evergreen boughs before Sam drew a bead on the head of an old cock who strutted an instant too long on his last spring's drumming log, and then verified the truth that pride goeth before a fall as he tossed up a flurry of leaves and snow in his death-struggle. So our hunter went on through this range of wooded hill, exhausting its present possibilities of game when he had killed another partridge, but all the while enjoying his solitary tramp. He heard the intermittent popping of the rifles at Hamner's, and in soliloquy mildly anathematized the shooters as "a pack o' dum'd fools." In a different spirit Joel Bartlett, hearing the frequent reports as he foddered his cattle in the barnyard, sighed loudly and sorrowfully, and said in the singsong tone that would now certainly be heard next day in the Fifth Day meeting, "A snare of the evil one, an' a-nother pitfall digged for the feet of the onwary! These men a-shootin' at innocent faowls of the air, is a-follerin' of a custom, an' a practyse, an' a observance o' them 'at hung Mary Dyer, an' grieviously pussecuted many formerly."

When Sam had come to the top of the hill the shortest way to the next likely hunting-ground lay past Hamner's, and a natural curiosity drew him to the shooting-ground.

Fortune had frowned on all the contestants but the amiable giant, Dart, who by his weight and good-nature and the possibly better gift of luck, seemed always to make his way, and having now got three turkeys Hamner was disposed to debar him from another chance. "I do' know haow on airth I'm a-goin' tu divide three turkeys 'mongst five on us," he said, " but I never was wuth a snap at figgers. Mebby Sary Ann 'll make hash on 'em." Luck, certainly not skill, had taken one of Joseph Hill's bullets into deadly contact with a turkey, and he, following Dart's hint, was telling his friends that M'ri would make a dumpling, the bird to be the core of the savory compound which would have been the stuffing of a larger turkey, "erless she took a notion tu fry it 'long wi' a slice o' pork, same as she would a patridge."

Poor Pelatiah was in doleful dumps, having fired three shots without getting a turkey, and now debating with himself whether he should hazard the remainder of his treasure on another. "I hit a nine-inch ring three times aout o' five, forty rod as I paced it up behind the barn t' hum, yist'd'y, wi' that gun," he confided to Sam, "Widder Wiggins's rifle, the best one the' is in Danvis, so ev'b'dy says, an' tu-day, Samwell, I can't hit a ten-acre lot!"

"It's fifty rod f'm here tu that box if it's a rod," said Sam to Pelatiah, and partly to himself. "The dum'd ol' cheatin' cuss! Look a here, Peltier, if you wanter try agin I'll pay for yer shot if it's a miss. Don't ye be in no hurry. You might," measuring the distance to the hill across the road with his eye, " you might forgit tu put any cap on, an' snap tew three times, an' then hol' high! Aim at the top o' 'Tater Hill 'f you'r a minter—'tain't nob'dy's business if your shot 's paid for. But don't ye graound your ball this side o' the turkey!"

"Goin', Mr. Lovel?" Hamner asked, as Sam shouldered his ponderous gun, known far and near as the "Ol' Ore Bed ;" "I was a-hopesin you 'd jine us."

"No," Sam replied ; "I can't hit a turkey forty rod off. I'm goin' up on your hill tu try 'f I c'n git another patridge. They 'pear tu be turrible scase t'day."

"Tell ye what, Lovel," said Dart, "I b'lieve Hamner's chick-a-biddied 'em all intu his barn wi' a ha' bushil o' buckwheat, an' sot 'em up for turkeys! These things we ben a-shootin' at is patridges, an' the scruff eends o' litters at that!"

"Re-freshmints up tu the hoe-tel, Mr. Lovel," Hamner said, taking no notice of these derogatory remarks. "Meant tu a-hed some austers, but I guess they hain't hed time to bring 'em raound sence it froze up."

"Was you thinkin' of importin' an auster up here, Hamner?" inquired the irrepressible Dart. "They don't bite, they say, in no month 'at hain't got an R in 't, an' the' hain't ben quite three sech, so the' hain't ben time tu move one up for ye, but I'd druther resk the chance o' gittin' one o' Hamner's turkeys at his forty rod, 'n tu try gittin' an auster aouten a plate o' his soup."

"Naow, *Mis*-ter Dart," Hamner asked, more in sorrow than in anger, "*du* you, *can* you expeck tu git a pailf'l o' solid meats aouten a plate o' austers at ninepunce a plate?"

Sam left the oyster question unsettled and made speedy way to the hill which overlooked the whole range.

Pelatiah bestowed his ungainly length upon the plank once more, and three times pulled the trigger with no responsive explosion of cap and charge. "G—o—s—h!" he exclaimed, with well-simulated surprise ; "I never thought tu put no cap on." This oversight having been duly remedied, at the next pull the Widder Wiggins's rifle responded with its wonted spiteful crack, which was more loudly repeated from the hill behind, and the turkey, with a few feeble flaps of its wings, sank upon the box.

"Sam Hill! What an e-cho!" Joseph ejaculated, taking in vain the name of a possible ancestor, and then looking toward the rough steep beyond the road he saw a thin film of smoke wafted upward through the evergreens. After one breathless moment of open-eyed and wide-mouthed wonder, he doubled himself up in a paroxysm of smothered laughter.

When the turkey was examined some one remarked that the "Widder Wiggins's rifle made a onaccaountable big hole," but Pelatiah bore home his prize in triumph and with unquestioned right.

IX.

SAM LOVEL'S THANKSGIVING.

As hunting was dearer to Sam Lovel than feasting, it very naturally happened that on the morning of the Thanksgiving Day to which Uncle Lisha had alluded, he was out on the hills with Drive rather than at home enduring the fuss and bustle of the " women folkses' " preparation of the great dinner. Such endurance he thought would be poorly paid for by all the good things that the feast would furnish forth, to be gorged at noon in a silent and business-like manner, as if to eat a little more than one's comfortable fill was the best, if not the only observance of the time-honored holiday that was required.

Sam was out betimes. As he took his way across the narrow fields to the woods, the dun grass land, the black squares and oblongs of fall ploughing, the gray of the deciduous trees, and the " black growth" of the woodlands were blurred together in the first light of the early morning, nothing distinct but lines and patches of the first snow, left by the ensuing warm days, and the serrated crest of the mountain now sharply cut against the Eastern sky. The hound, quartering the way toward sunrise, came into sight and vanished, now to the right, now to the left, first white spots and then a dimly-defined dog, then white spots and no dog, nor any indication of his nearness but his loud snuffing and the crisp crush of the frosty herbage under his feet. Presently he gave tongue on a cold scent, and puzzling out with his miraculous gift of smell the devious course of the fox over knolls and through swales of matted mouse-haunted wild grass, and by and by, when daylight had set well-defined bounds to field and forest, led his slowly-following master to the ridge of the first hill. Then the sun began to burn its way up the sky with so intense a flame that it seemed to be consuming the stubby trunks and low-spread branches of the stunted evergreens bristling in blurred silhouette on the mountain crest. Sam followed the trend of the long ledge that formed the top of the hill, a sheer steep abutting toward the West, a long rough slope slanting to a dark gorge on the East. Out of this came from time to time the tuneful baying of the hound as he worked southward on the scent, so cold that only in those places that held it best it greeted his nostrils with an aroma strong enough to bring forth his bugle-like challenge. The intervals of silence became longer between the bugle notes, sounding now fainter and farther away, till at last unheard at all, though the murmur of a mountain brook changing with wafts of the light breeze, the monotonous song of the evergreens swelling and falling with its varying touch, and a hundred nameless mysterious voices of the woods fooled the hunter's ear now and then. But he had an abiding faith that at last Drive would get up the fox and bring him back along this ridge, and so he listened and waited, sitting on a moss-cushioned log while all the chickadees of the neighborhood came and visited him with inquisitive friendliness, and the jays, at more respectful distance, squalled a protest against his intrusion on their haunts. A solitary crow, belated in his migration, discovered the silent and motionless figure, and made as much pother as if it had been a featherless owl or a furless fox; but when his clamor failed to bring any response from the brethren now far beyond the sound of his voice, he flapped away in silent disgust. A red squirrel scampering over the matted leaves in quest of buried treasure sat up at the toe of Sam's boot, and after a short inspection of this queer black stump ventured on to it, and then as far as Sam's knee, whence a wink of the hunter's gray eye frightened him in a sudden panic, from which he recovered sufficiently when he had gained the vantage of a tree trunk to rattle out a volley of abuse. When these visitors had all departed and Sam had listened long in vain, he moved on to a bald peak of the hill from which a portion of the valley could be seen, with its cleared fields and wooded cobbles, and farm houses and outbuildings strung along the frozen black road like nests on a slender leafless branch. Some were as deserted to-day as the vireo's nest that hung in a fork of the witch-hazel beside him, the inmates away for one day's thanksgiving as the birds were for months of it. But from the chimney of one red-painted homestead, which Sam's wandering glances always came back to, a banner of smoke flaunted, denoting occupancy.

"Someb'dy stayin' t' hum t' Pur'n't'ns," he soliloquized. "Guess most on 'em 's gone some' eres tu Thanksgivin', f' the' hain't nob'dy stirrin' 'round aou' door. Guess they hain't keepin' on 't there, for 'f they was ol' Granther Pur'n't'n's shay 'ould be a-loomin' up 'long side o' the barn like a tew storey haouse afire. Wonder 'f the' hain't nob'dy t' hum, 'n' the dum'd haouse is afire"—as the chimney belched forth a greater volume of smoke. "Do' know but what I'd better go an' see. That 'ere fox is an ol' N' Hampsh'r traveller, an' he'll tow Drive clean t' the C'net'cut River 'fore he gives it up an' comes back, an' I'll be dum'd 'f I'm a-goin' to set 'raound here a-waitin' for him 'till t'morrer night. I b'lieve that dum'd ol' haouse *is* afire!" And listening one moment more for the voice of the hound, almost afraid that he might hear it, he started down the sheer hillside, checking now and then his headlong course with clutches on bushes, saplings, and tree-trunks, till he reached the level of the alder-bordered brook that wound along the base of the hill. The red winter berries glowed there in vain to catch his eye, and he crushed unseen beneath his feet the scarlet cones of the wild turnip drooping on their withered stalks as he breasted the tangled sprawl of the alders. When beyond them he came in sight of the house again, he caught a glimpse of a trim figure as the kitchen door opened for an instant, the flash of a dish-pan and the glitter of its discharged contents, and a few notes of a clear voice singing, "The Girl I Left Behind Me." The figure and the voice made his heart beat quicker, but he slackened his pace as he taxed his wits for an excuse for his call. When he crossed the chips in front of the woodshed, he had decided that his first idea was the best to act upon, and that if he did not quite believe it now, he really had believed that the house was on fire. He knocked at the kitchen door and waited long enough for flames to have made great headway, while he listened to the voice singing with all the freedom from embarrassment of one who sings without a listener, and for the singer's sole pleasure—

> "If ever I chance to go that way,
>   And she has not resigned me,
> I'll reconcile my mind and stay
>   With the girl I left behind me."

He did not knock again till the words ended and the singer began to hum the tune in a lower voice. Then the singing and the accompanying clatter of dishes and swash of "wrench water" suddenly stopped, and Sam knew that in the ensuing hush Huldah was wiping her hands on the towel behind the buttery door, that the few quick footsteps took her to the looking-glass in the door of the clock, whose ticking he could now hear, and now she was coming. When she opened the door such a bright pleased surprise shone on her pretty face that he could compare it to nothing but the brightness of that morning's sunrise.

"Why, good land sakes alive! Samwell Lovel, where on airth did you come from?"

"Wal," said Sam, his cheeks as red as hers, "I was a-huntin' up on Pig's Back, an' I seen the smoke a-tumblin' aouten your chimbly at sech a rate 't I was afeared the haouse was afire. I thought most likely 'at you'd all gone off t' Thanksgivin', an' suthin' nuther hed ketched, an' so I come ri' daown. I'm sorry 't I troubled ye, but I'm dreffle glad 't the' hain't nothin' afire. Guess I'll be a-goin' naow."

"Why, what's yer hurry, Mr. Lovel? Come in an' seddaown an' rest ye a spell. Aour folks is all gone, father 'n' mother 'n' Sis, up to Gran'ther's, an' lef' nob'dy t' hum but me 'n' the cat. I didn't keer no gret 'baout goin', an' so I staid t' hum to keep haouse. Come in an' seddaown a minute, won't ye? while I gwup stairs an' look o' that sto'pipe—it *hes* ben kinder aouter kilter. Come in an' take a cheer. The kitchin looks like all git aout" [it was as neat as a new bandbox], "but I wa'n't 'spectin' nob'dy, an' the' hain't no fire in the square room. I'd take yer gun, but I dassent—set it in the corner, er heng it up on the hooks over the mantel-tree there. Father's gun's gone t' V'gennes, a-bein' altered over tu a—a cap-lock, is 't you call 'em? He thinks they're better 'n flint-locks. Du you think they be, Sa—Mr. Lovel, I mean?"

"Wal, they be handier an' sartiner to go off, but I do' know but what a flint-lock gun is 'baout as good—to heng up, as yer father's does mostly," Sam answered, looking up contemplatively at the hooks where his own gun now hung.

"Make yerself t' hum, Samwell—why, haow I du keep a-callin' on ye by yer fust name! excuse me, *Mr.* Lovel —while I gwup an' see 'baout that 'ere sto'pipe."

The stovepipe must have been found in satisfactory condition, for Huldah presently reappeared in a smart new calico gown, and with her hair neatly brushed and fastened with a high tortoise-shell comb.

"Is it usuil, Mr. Lovel," she asked, after she had set away her dishes, and drawing a chair to the stove, sat down and folded her hands in seemly fashion over her check apron, "for folks to knock at the door when they think a haouse is afire?"

"I wa'n't a-knockin'!" Sam said, dropping his abashed eyes from her roguish glance, "I was a-beginnin'—kinder mawdret, ye know, to bust open the door. I didn't wanter skeer nob'dy, s'posin' the' was anyb'dy t'hum, which I hedn't no idee the' was."

Huldah could not help laughing at this absurd explanation, nor could Sam help joining her, and when they had had their laugh out they found themselves much more at ease and became very sociable. When Huldah again corrected herself for addressing him by his first name, he reminded her of their old school days when she had never thought of calling him anything but Sam. "We was putty good frien's them times, Huldy, but I'm afeard you hain't a-feelin' so frien'ly tow-wards me naow, a-Misterin' on me so. I do' know who folks is a-talkin' tu when they says *Mis*ter Lovel; seem's 's 'ough they was mistakin' on me for father or gran'ther."

"Wal, then, Sam, 'f 't suits ye any better!" cried Huldah; and he declared that it did suit him better, "a dum'd sight."

"I hedn't made no cal'lations on gittin' a reg'lar dinner tu-day, bein' 'at the' wa'n't nob'dy here but me," Huldah apologized, looking up at the clock as it warned for eleven. "I'm dreffle sorry 't I didn't naow, but I'm a-goin' t' git ye some nutcakes an' pie an' cheese, an' you'll hafter stay yer stomerk wi' them. You mus' be hungrier 'n a bear, eatin' of your breakfas' 'fore daylight, I s'pose, an' a-traipsin' raound in the woods all the fo'noon," and she bustled away to prepare the lunch, in spite of Sam's protesting that he "wa'n't the least mite hungry, an' 'ould druther set an' talk 'n t' eat."

"It does beat all natur'," she said, with an emphatic and rather petulant toss of her head, as she returned from the pantry with a pie and a plate of doughnuts, "'at any body can enj'y traipsin' raound, up-hill an' daown, all day long, arter a leetle insi'nificant fox! An' shoolin' an' stumblin' raound the lots all night arter coons! Ketch me, 'f I was a man. But you men folks du beat all creation!"

"Shouldn't wonder 'f we did, putty nigh, 'xceptin' the womern part on't. That beats us all holler. But I'd a good deal druther ketch ye jest as ye be. I hain't hed a chance tu speak tu ye 'lone 'fore in a dawg's age!"

"I do' know 'f nothin' 'at the' 's ben t' hender, 'f ye wanted tu," Huldah said, pouting her red lips, "erless you'd forgot where we lived. You hain't ben a-nigh f'r I d' know haow long, an' ye wouldn't t'day 'f you hedn't a-thought the haouse was afire 'n' nob'dy t' hum," and the pout changed to a smile.

"If I c'ld raly b'lieve 'at the time seemed long sence I'd ben here t' anyb'dy but me, I sh'ld be turrible glad on 't, an' the' wouldn't be no need o' settin' the haouse afire t' fetch me. But ye see, Huldy, yer father he don't set no gret by folks 'at goes a-huntin', no more 'n his darter does, 'n' so I hain't felt ezackly free 'baout comin'."

"Why, Samwill! I wa'n't sayin' 'at I hed anythin' agin folkses huntin'; I was on'y wonderin' what makes 'em lufter."

"Wal, it's kinder natur', I s'pose, borned inter some on us, same's 't is inter haoun' dawgs, an' we can't help a-runnin' off int' the woods. Suthin' takes us. An' when 't 'ain't none tew pleasant for a feller t' hum, like 'nough he goes off a-huntin' er a-fishin' oftener 'n he would 'f 'twas pleasant. Naow, 'f I hed a haouse o' my own an' someb'dy t' keep it—wal, say as this is kep'," looking around the neat kitchen with a look of admiration that grew as it returned and lingered on the bright face of the young housekeeper, "an' wa'n't allus a-scoldin' an' findin' fault, I p'sume to say I wouldn't go a-huntin' more'n onct a week in the season on't, 'thaout 'twas when oncommon good days come oncommon often."

"The' hain't no daoubt," Huldah said, rising in some confusion, and taking the tea-kettle from the back of the stove, going out to fill it, talking back through the open door as she went to the pump,, "but what you c'ld *hire* someb'dy nuther to keep haouse for ye"—then the squeaking and gurgling crescendo of the pump's voice drowned hers. "I'm a-goin' t' make ye a cup o' tea," returning with the kettle and setting it on the stove, and giving the fire an enlivening punch.

"I wa'n't a-meanin' no *hired* help," Sam said—" no, don't make me no tea—I'd druther you wouldn't take no sech trouble—no, not no hired help, but some b'dy 'at 'ould —'at thought they could stan' it tu—tu go snucks along wi' me a-ownin' of a haouse, an' keepin' on it for me an' her."

"Why, Samwell Lovell! Haow you du go on! Did anybody ever!" cried Huldah, glowing with blushes. Then she held her breath to hear what, she was sure, her lover now must ask. But Sam was frightened into dumbness by his own unwonted boldness; and at last when the silence was becoming painfully awkward, she not knowing what else to say, broke it with the unfortunate remark that "The' was some other nat'ral borned hunter up on the hill, she guessed, for she hearn a haoun' dawg a-yollupin' up there." Sam hurried out to listen, and she followed him.

"Wal, by the gret horn spoon!" he exclaimed, as the familiar long-drawn notes of his own hound struck his ear, "I'll be dum'd if that hain't Drive, as sure as shootin'! He's brung that 'ere fox back f'm the Lord knows where! Yes, sir," as the musical cry swelled louder from the nearest ridge, "he's jest a-shovin' on him, 'n' he's a-goin' t' cross by the Butt'nuts, 'n' I b'lieve I c'n head him!"

Sam was in the kitchen and out again with his gun in an instant and speeding across the fields toward the well-known runway, where three great butternut-trees crowned a knoll with a widespread of thick, ungraceful ramage. Sweetheart and doughnuts were forsaken, love almost forgotten and hunger quite, in the ardor of the chase, though it must be said in palliation of Sam's abrupt departure that he longed to give Huldah an exhibition of his skill as a hunter, to shoot the fox before her eyes and presently bring her the furry trophy of his prowess. But alas for his hopes! Before he was within the longest possible gunshot of the knoll he saw the fox crossing it, halting for a moment to look back at the bellowing hound, and then disappearing with undulating lopes on his way to the western range. He would probably play when he reached those lines of ledges, Sam thought, and after a little hesitation and more than one wistful glance back to the red house, he went forward. He was ashamed to return now, so unsuccessful.

"My!" Huldah said to herself, as with her plump hand shading her eyes she watched the receding form of her lover, "I hope to goodness he'll git him!" Then when the fox appeared and disappeared far out of Sam's reach, she exhaled her long-held breath in a great sigh, not wholly of disappointment. "Wal, I don't care, he'll come back naow." But when he went on with a swinging stride that speedily took him out of her sight, her eyes filled with tears of vexation. "The 'tarnal great fool! I hope 't he won't never come a-nigh me agin 's long 's I live an' breathe, an' I hope 't that won't be long—I do! What a plegged fool I was t' up an' tell o' hearin' a haoun'! I wish 't the' wa'n't a haoun' dawg ner a fox in this wide-livin' world for men t' go shoolin' an' runnin' an' traipsin' arter when they might be a-duin' suthin' wuth while. He cares more for a mis'able sneakin' fox 'n he does for me, or anything on airth, to run off arter one an' leave me jest when—I wish 't *I* was a fox, an' then mebby—Oh ! wouldn't I keep him a-moggin' a spell—I won't never speak to him agin so long 's I live an' breathe ! Let him hev his ol' haoun' an' his foxes an' his hateful ol' gun an' his everlastin' huntin' 'f he likes 'em better 'n he does me. I don't care, so there, naow !" But she was choking with alternating tearful fits of sorrow and anger all the afternoon, and when her father and mother and little sister returned from the Thanksgiving at "gran'thers," they wondered to find her so woebegone.

"I hedn't no idee," said her father to her mother after furtively watching her as he sat warming his hands at the stove, "'at Huldy keered a row o' pins 'baout goin' t' father's."

When miles away on one of the farthest ridges of the western hills, Sam at sundown shot his fox, and gave the dying brute a spiteful if merciful finishing kick in the head, he said, "Blast yer pictur', I wish 't you hed ha' gone clean t' N' Hampsh'r', 'n I never 'd see er heard on ye, dum ye ! You've cost me more 'n any fox ever cost a man afore sen the' was foxes an' men an' women folks in this world !" He bore an aching heart for many a weary day before he forgave himself or was forgiven by Huldah.

One day in the winter Huldah came to Aunt Jerusha on an errand. "I wanter borry your wool caards, Aunt Jerushy, to caard some rolls for father some socks. Aourn is lent, we do' know where." In the conversation that accompanied the borrowing and lending of the cards, Aunt Jerusha asked when Huldah had seen Samwill Lovel, to which Huldah replied with a show of spitefulness that her wistful eyes belied, that she had not seen him since about

Thanksgiving Day, "an' didn't wanter, as she knowed on!" Whereat Aunt Jerusha was surprised and grieved, for it was her cherished hope that these two, her favorites among all the young folks of Danvis, would some day make a match. After some coaxing Huldah told her old friend her grievance, and so Uncle Lisha came to know in part the story of Sam's Thanksgiving.

X.

LITTLE SIS.

"Good Lord o' massy! if I hain't jest abaout clean tuckered aout!" Mrs. Purington gasped, exhaling a long-drawn sigh as she dropped her portly person into a creaking splint-bottom chair in her own kitchen, then flopped her sun-bonnet into her short lap, and stroked the hair back with both hands from her heated brow. "Whew! 't 't ain't hot, jest a-roastin', bilin' hot! Huldy, reach me a dipper o' water, won't ye? I'm e'en a'most choked. I sot that ere pitcher o' emptin's on the winder stool; you ta' keer on em, won't ye?" Huldah brought her mother a quart dipper full of cool water from the pump, that with its dolorous squeaks and hollow groans always reminded her now of last year's Thanksgiving Day.

"Lord o' massy! I b'lieve I *be* roasted," Mrs. Purington exclaimed, regarding her scarlet reflection in the bright interior of the tin dipper, after she had taken a long draught. "Wal," she said, after resting the dipper on her knee, and wiping her face with a corner of her apron, "I've ben all 'raound Robin Hood's barn tu borry them emptin's. Fust I went tu Joel's, though I might ha' knowed better 'n tu, for Jemimy she allers uses milk risin'; mis'able flat-tasted bread it makes tew. Ketch me a-makin' bread wi' milk risin'! Then arter I'd sot an' talked wi' Jemimy a spell—Joel, he's got a '*consarn*' a-workin' on his mind, an' he's a-goin' off on a preachin' taower jes' 's soon 's they get through hayin'. Shouldn't wonder a mite 'f he did afore if the weather happens tu come on ketchin'; 'n' like 's not 't will, for dog days hain't over yit, an' nob'dy never knows what the weather 's a-goin' t' be in dog-days. The idear o' goin' shoolin' off wi' one o' his '*consarns*,' leavin' her an' them child'n an' the farm tu 'tend tu ! Ketch me a-marryin' a Quaker, 'at's allus lierble tu be took with a '*consarn*' ! Arter I sot an' talked wi' Jemimy a spell I went on tu Briggses; but Miss' Briggs she hain't got nothin' but yeast-cakes, an' I hain't uster usin' them. So arter I'd sot an' rested me a spell—she's got a new quilt on the frames—pretty time o' year tu be a-quiltin'—sunflower patch-work it is, an' 'll look c'nsid'able scrumptious when 't 's done. I went on tu Hillses,' an' Miss' Hill she'd jest sot a mess tu workin', 'n' so she hedn't got none. Jozeff he's a-hayin' on 't, arter his fashion ! Then I went along over tu Uncle Lisher's, an' there I made aout tu git me some emptin's. Uncle Lisher he's jes' fairly got tu hayin' on 't, hain't ben begun more'n tew three days. Tom Hamlin he 's a helpin' on him—payin' up his shoemakin', like 's not. They've just hed a letter f'm George aout tu the 'Hio. Says crops is lookin' well in the 'Hio, an' he's a-duin' well, an' wants 'em both to come aout there an' live 'long wi' him. I don't scasely b'lieve they ever will, but I do' know. They're a-gettin' 'long in years, an' it's a turrible ways off. Why, that letter was wrote the last o' June or fo' part o' July, an' here it is the middle of August! Wal," taking another draught from the dipper, and making slow preparations to rise, "we've got us some emptin's tu start with, an naow we've got tu set tu work an' make some. Hope yer father won't tip over the pot agin, pokin' raound in the suller. You've skum the milk, I s'pose, an' got the pans washed an' scalded?"

"Yes," Huldah answered from the sink, where she stood washing and peeling potatoes.

"You be dreffle mumpin' this summer," said her mother, after waiting a little for her to speak further. "It's jest yis an' no with ye, an' ye never laugh ner sing a mite 's ye uster. I b'lieve I'd orter steep up some boneset an' hev ye take some; *I* b'lieve yer stomerk 's aouten order."

"Why, mother, I'm jest as tough as a bear," Huldah declared, blushing and making a brave effort to laugh; she could not help smiling at the thought of boneset as a remedy for her ill—heartsease would be more to the purpose, it seemed to her.

"It is a turrible job tu fix them ol' pertaters fit for cookin'," said Mrs. Purington, now apparently just noticing her daughter's occupation. "Seem 's 'ough we'd ort tu hev some new ones by this time. Wonder 'f yer father 's dug int' any hills tu see? Where's Sis?" she asked, after looking thoughtfully at Huldah and the potatoes as she went to hang the dipper and sun-bonnet on their respective nails. "I hain't seen nor hearn nothin' on her sen I come in." It was indeed noticeable that the six-year-old pet of the household had not even in so short a time in a wakeful forenoon in some way made her whereabouts known, and her mother wondered now with a maternal qualm of conscience that she had not sooner remarked the absence of the child's voice, talking to herself, or asking endless unanswerable questions, or singing her rag doll to imaginary sleep. She suddenly realized how still it was, that there was no sound in the kitchen but the buzzing of the flies, the ticking of the clock, and the fluttering splash and chip, chip of the potato washing and paring, and that from outdoors came no sound but the lazy "crating" of the hens, the dolorous mixture of peep and cluck wherewith the half-grown chickens expressed their contentment, the dry clap of a locust's wings, followed by his long, shrill cry when he had lighted in the chip-littered yard, and from farther off the faint ringing of the mowers' whetted scythes.

"Why," said Huldah, coming with a start out of a maze of troubled thoughts, " she was a-tewin' 'raound an' a-pesterin' me half tu death 'baout this an' that she wanted t' du, an' at last I gi'n her her little baskit 'at—'at she thinks so much on, an' tol' her she might gwup in the stump lot a-blackbaryin' a spell. I tol' her she mustn't gwaout o' sight o' the haouse."

"Wal," Mrs. Purington said, looking out toward the hills, "I guess you hedn't orter let her. I d' know 's she'd orter gwup there 'lone. She'd better ben a-watchin' the ol' hen turkey an' her young uns. If they git up tu the aidge of the woods the foxes 'll ketch every identical one on 'em. Oh dear me suz! Seems 's 'ough the pleggid foxes hed ort tu git some scaser, wi' Sam Lovel an' mongst 'em a-huntin' an' a-haounin' on 'em half the year; but they don't. Seems 's 'ough that young un ort tu be some'eres in sight er a-comin' hum by this time. Haow long's she ben gone?"

"She's ben gone," Huldah answered, looking at the clock—"why, it's most an hour an' a half! Mother, 'f you'll put the pertaters in the kittle, I'll go an' git her. 'F I don't git back soon 'nough, the pork 's all cut an' in the fryin'-pan ready for fresh-nin'." So putting on her sun-bonnet she went out, her mother following to the door to say, " Jes' 's like 's not she's over in the medder 'long wi' yer father 'n' the rest on 'em." With this hope Huldah went out toward the meadow till she could see her father and the two hired men swinging their scythes with even strokes, but there was no little sister there, and she went on quickly, crossing the brook where its summer-shrunken current wimpled among the stones in the shade of a thicket of young firs. She saw a print of a small shoe in the soft gravel, half filled with water, and pointing toward the berry lot. Surely, she thought, she must soon find her now, and listened a moment with the expectation of hearing the child prattling to herself or rustling among the bushes. But she heard nothing but the hum of insects, the chirp of crickets, and an occasional bird note, and calling, got no answer. But she must see her presently, for it was impossible to keep out of sight in the field that the axe had swept all tree growth from only two years ago. But when she entered it, after beating along its lower edge for a while, she was surprised to see how tall the sprouts and bushes had grown since she had last been there. It now seemed hopeless enough to look here for one grown to full stature, much more so to find a child whose head would be overtopped by the lowest of the blackberry brambles that reared themselves with rampant growth about every blackened stump and log heap.

Perhaps Polly had fallen asleep on some inviting bed of moss by the brook. Nothing was likelier, and it was strange she had not sooner thought of it. Returning, she followed all the turns of the little watercourse along the border of the stump lot, but saw no living thing she caredto ; nothing but a scared trout flashing across the shadows of a pool ; heard nothing but the warning cry of a mother partridge and the startling whir of wings when the old bird and her well-grown brood burst away in brief flight, and then the lisping call that gathered the scattered family. Why would not her little chick of a sister hear and answer her call ? Huldah went back into the brush and swiftly threaded the maze of cowpaths, and with laborious climbing gained the tops of the tallest stumps, whose height showed how deep the snow was when the trees were felled, and scanned all the thickets she could overlook, always hoping to see somewhere among the tangle of stalks and leafage the little pink sun-bonnet moving about. Once she thought she had surely caught sight of it, but on approach it proved to be only the full-flowered spike of a willow herb nodding to the breeze or bending under the shifting weight of the bees. She called loudly and often, but was answered only by the mewing of a catbird that flitted near yet unseen in the thickets, and by the sudden jangle of a cowbell as its startled wearer crashed away through the brush. Sometimes the mysterious murmurs of the forest would fool her ear for a moment ; then when she listened they seemed to come from everywhere and could be located nowhere. One moment she was so vexed and impatient that if she had come upon the little wanderer her first impulse would have been to give her a scolding ; the next she was choking with a swelling ache of dread that she would have given the world to have cured by a sight of the yellow-polled pet and tease, whom if she might but find alive and well she would never scold again. So she hurried on in her fruitless search till she came to the upper end of the half-cleared field where the lofty branches of the great trees linteled the doorway of the ancient forest, whose depths and darkness and mystery she feared, but would dare to enter, if there was one promised chance of her finding the lost child there. Yes, lost. The fact with all its terrible possibilities forced itself upon her, and horrible visions floated in a swiftly returning procession before her misty eyes of the little form lying dead at the foot of a precipice, or drowned in a brook pool, or torn by wild beasts, or at best stumbling blindly onward in a craze of fright perhaps to a worse death by starvation and terror. It would be only a waste of precious time for her to go into the woods. There was nothing for her to do but to hasten home and rouse the neighborhood for the search. She mounted a great boulder for one more unrewarded look, and to make another unanswered call. She could see her home basking in the August sun with such a restful air as if it was never to shelter the sorrow that was soon to enter it; and a wood thrush filled the cloisters of the woods with his sweet chime of silver bells as if there were naught but peace and happiness in their quiet depths. Huldah was no saint, and she felt an angry resentment of this mockery of her trouble. She could have wrung the thrush's neck to end the song so ill-attuned to her feelings, and it would have been a slight relief to see some token of disturbance about the house, though it would not have quieted her self-reproach. If this wrathful feeling had not been overpowered by the stronger emotion of grief before she reached home, it might have been somewhat appeased by the pervading air of anxiety that brooded over the household.

Her father, watching for her as he smoked his after-dinner pipe, came out to meet her, questioning her with a troubled face. She only halted to say in a choked voice, "O father, she's lost! Hurry, an' raout aout everybody!" and answered the inquiring look of the hired men who stopped their meditative whittling and arose from the doorstep at her approach with, "Polly's lost! Go an' tell 'em all tu come an' find her!" Her mother, meeting her at the door, heard this, and retreating to the nearest chair, sat down, spreading a helpless hand on either knee. "Oh dear me suz! Huldy, I don't see haow on airth you ever, ever come tu let her go!"

"O mother, *don't!* Is the' any tea left? I'm a-chokin', an' tuckered." She poured out a cupful from the teapot, swallowed it at a draught, and went quickly out. "I'm a-goin' tu Joel's an' Solon's an' Hillses' an' that way 's fur 's I can tu tell 'em," she said to her father, who was hurriedly consulting with the men. "You an' John an' Lije go t' other ways. I searched and hollered all over the stump lot, an' never seen nothin' on her but her track where she crossed the brook, a-goin'," and she hastened down the road.

"Thee don't say so!" Jemima Bartlett said, her placid face full of pity when Huldah briefly told her errand. "The poor little precious! I'll call the men folks right off up aouten the medder. They'll come tu rights when they hear the horn. Thee 'd better come in an' sed daown an' rest thee a spell, thee does look so beat aout, poor child!"

But Huldah sped on while the blasts of the conch-shell were echoing from the hills, and when she looked back as she turned into Solon Briggs's yard, she saw

Joel and his hired man trudging along the road toward her home.

Solon happened to be mending his "hay-riggin'," and, dropping his tools on the door-yard chips, he hastened away as soon as he heard her message, stopping only to ask if it would be "more essifactious for him tu go an' help her raise a human cry?"

Joseph Hill came to the door in his stockings trying to rub and gape away the left-over sleepiness of an after-dinner nap. When he had slowly pulled on his boots he was ready to go; he hardly knew which way till he had "told M'ri," who came with the youngest baby in her arms, and two a-foot tugging at her skirts and peeping from behind them, while she offered her condolences. The whistling growl of Gran'ther Hill came from where he sat in his arm-chair at the back door, asking many questions: "What is 't yer a-talkin' 'baout, M'rier? Somebody lost? Who is it? Purin't'ns' young un? Don't Purin't'ns' folks know no better 'n tu let a baby gwoff int' the woods? Why didn't they chuck her int' the cist'n? Then they 'd ha' knowed where she was! Wal, I s'pose we all got tu turn aout an' sarch arter her," and he came stamping through the house with his hat on and his cane in his hand. "You needn't talk to me, M'rier!" he said, glowering fiercely at his daughter-in-law when she mildly protested against his going, "I hain't ol', nuther, I tell ye. Eighty-five year hain't nothin' tu a man 'at's ben where I ben, when the's babies lost in the woods! I've tracked Injins, an' I guess I c'n track a foolish little young un!" and he marched off with his son with as much alacrity as he had responded to Ethan Allen's call in the long past May of his youth.

Presently Huldah was at Uncle Lisha's telling her sympathizing old friend, Aunt Jerusha, of the loss of the child, and she added, as she had not before, "It's all my fault—I let her go a-baryin'!" The old man was in the shop mending a piece of harness, and the door between the shop and the house being open, as it usually was when he had no visitors, his ears caught the girl's voice and something of her story.

"Good airth an' seas! Huldy, what's that you're a-sayin'? Sissy lost? Haow? Where?" he shouted as he suddenly appeared in the doorway with the tug in his hand. Then she told him all she could, repeating that it was all her fault, for she found a little comfort in making this confession now.

"Wal," pitching the tug back into the shop, and untying his apron and sloughing it off on the threshold, "I'll go an' du what I can. I c'n waddle 'raound in the woods arter a fashion, an' I c'n holler c'nsid'able, an' I tell ye hollerin' caounts sech times. Fust I'll go an' holler fer Tawmus. Say, Huldy, I'll tell ye," he said, turning toward her while one upstretched hand groped along the pegs for his hat, "the's one man in Danvis 'at I druther hev a-sarchin' for Sissy 'an all the hull caboodle on us, ol' an' young, big an' little. He knows the woods julluk a book, an' c'n read every sign in 'em—an' that 'ere man is Samwill Lovel! You're spryer 'n I be, 'n' some spryer 'n Jerushy, I guess. You cut over to his haouse an' start him!"

"O Uncle Lisher, I *can't!*" Huldah gasped, her hot, tired face paling an instant, then burning redder with blushes, "I can't! Someb'dy else 'll tell him. You go an' tell him!"

"I tell ye, Huldy, *you* mus' go! The' hain't no time for me tu turkle over there, an' you comin' this way they'll depend on your tellin' on him! Good airth an' seas! gal, this hain't no time for stinkin' pride 'f you *be* aout with him. He'd sarch tu the eend o' the airth if you ast him—he warships the graound you tread! Go right stret, an' clipper, tew!" and having got his hat on he took her by the shoulders and gently pushed her outdoors, and as far as the gate, facing her the desired way. She went on, accelerating her pace till she was running when she came to the door of the Lovel homestead, caring for nothing now so much as the finding of her lost sister.

Mrs. Lovel, Sam's stepmother, a gaunt, hard featured woman, came to the open door, beating the threshold with a broom to frighten away some intruding chickens. "Shoo! you pesterin' torments! I wish 't the aigs o' yer breed was destr'yed! Why, massy sakes alive! Huldy Pur'n't'n! What be you in sech a pucker 'baout?" she cried in astonishment when Huldah's swift approach diverted her attention from the objects of her displeasure. "Why, you look 's 'ough you'd ben dragged through a brush heap, an' scairt aouten your seben senses!"

"Oh, Miss' Lovell, Polly 's lost in the woods. Where's Samwell? I want him tu help find her. Where is he?"

"Polly lost!" Mrs. Lovell repeated, regarding Huldah with a reproachful severity in her countenance that the poor girl felt she deserved. "Up back o' your haouse? Wal, I shouldn't wonder a mite 'f you never faound her a-livin'. Like 's anyways she'll tumble off 'm the rocks an' break her neck, 'f the' don't suthin' nuther ketch her afore. Some on 'em was a-tellin' o' hearin' a wolf a-haowlin' an' a-haowlin' t' other night, an' some thinks the' 's a painter a-hantin' 'raound. The' 's allus bears, an' they du say 'at the' hain't nothin' 'at bears likes better' t' eat 'n child'n. There 's them young ones 'at sassed Lijer, wan't it? Ye know the' was three bears, on'y jest three, come aouten the woods an' eat forty on 'em!"

Huldah, rejecting such consolation with raised hands and averted face, asked again for Sam.

"Sam! Humph! Sure 'nough, where is he? You tell. Him an' his father finished up hayin' yist'd'y, an' of course he hed tu put off a bee-huntin' the fust thing arter breakfus' this mornin'; nob'dy knows which way. He'd a 'tarnal sight better ben a-fencin' the stacks so 't the kyows c'ld be turned int' the medder. An' Lovel, he's a-putterin' 'raound daown in the back lot 'baout suthin' 't hain't no vally, I'll warrant. O my eyes an' Betty Martin! If these men hain't 'nough tu drive any womern distracted! Haow ol' *was* Polly?" as if the bright little life was assuredly ended.

"Six, the twenty fourth o' June," Huldah answered, and turning away went wearily homeward, half the hope dying out of her heart, now that there was no hope of finding Sam.

When Joel Bartlett arrived he went in and shook hands with Mrs. Purington as solemnly as he performed the same ceremony when he "broke the meetin'" on First and Fifth Days. "I wanter tell thee, Mary Pur'n't'n, tu keep quiet in thy mind," he said. "Aour Heavenly Father, withaout whose knowledge not a sparrer falls tu the graound, will ta' keer of a precious little child; an' I feel it bore in upon me 'at thy little darter will be restored tu thee. Sech poor insterments as we be o' His'n, we will du aour best indivors. An' naow, Mary, keep quiet in thy mind, an' seek for stren'th in Him tu help thee tu bear this grievious trial o' waitin' on His will."

The rescue party had been quickly mustered, and the plan of search agreed upon. It heartened Huldah when she reached home to know that twenty-five or thirty stalwart men were already ranging the woods in quest of her lost sister, all so inspired with neighborly kindness that they would spare themselves no pain or hardship in the search.

But oh, if the keenest and bravest woodsman among all these hills were only on the same quest! Why of all the days in the year must he have chosen this most anxious one of a lifetime wherein to go bee-hunting? Huldah mentally relegated the bees to that limbo whither she had long before in like manner banished the foxes.

XI.

SAM LOVEL'S BEE-HUNTING.

Away up on the mountain-side, where some hopeful pioneer had hewn out of the wilderness a few acres with slight and remote possibilities of a future pasture, Sam Lovel was wallowing at noon among the golden rods, willow-herbs, and asters that filled this wild garden with yellow and pink and blue and white bloom, yet more varied with the heightening and deepening of their colors by sunlight and shadow, and contrast. The bees were making the most of such bountiful pasturage; the clearing droned with their incessant hum, and the drowsy murmur of their toil seemed to have lulled the forest to sleep, so still were all its depths. Sam had no trouble to imprison one of the busy horde in his bee-box, but more to line his liberated captive and the mates returning with her, for the little square of sunlit sky was flecked with hundreds of hurrying brown specks. But his sharp eyes were not easily foiled when he set them fairly to their work, and he had not lain long on his back among the ferns before he caught the airy trail of the bees that carried their burdens of sweets from his box, set on the nearest tall stump. He did not follow far into the woods before he found the great tree where they were hoarding their wealth. "Tu easy faound for fun," he said, as he lighted his pipe and began to cut his initials on the trunk of the old maple, "but bee-huntin' 's better 'n no huntin', an' more fun 'n fencin' stacks 'at c'n jes' 's well wait a spell while the rowen grows, er a-hearin' everlastin' tewin' an' scoldin'. An' it helps tol'able well ter keep a feller's mind off 'm onprofitable thinkin'. Wal, there you be, Mister L.," slowly pushing his knife shut against his thigh as he critically regarded his carving, " an' you 're the best letter I got in my name, for the' 's an l in Huldy. I sh'd like tu put tew more on ye in her'n. Ho hum! Wal, come, you dum'd ol' long-laigged fool of a S. L., le's go an' find another bee tree." And he took himself back to the clearing. He captured a bee on the first " yaller top" he came to, and soon established another line, but it took much longer to trace it to the bee's home, and when he had set his mark on this, it was time to be going to his own home. He took his unerring course through the pathless woods, stopping now and then to rest on a log or knoll that seemed to be set with its cushion of moss on purpose for him. During one of these halts, when half way through the woods, he heard a cry, so strange that he paused to listen for a repetition of it while his lighted match went out before it reached his pipe, or the pipe his mouth. Once more the distressful wail struck his ear, whether far away or only faint and near he could not tell. " Wal," letting out his held breath and striking another match, " 'f I've got another painter on my hands, I wish 't I hed the ol' Ore Bed 'long. But like 'nough 'tain't nothin' but a bluejay 'at's struck a new noise — I thought they hed 'em all a'ready, though." And he went on, pausing a little at times to listen to and locate the voice, which presently ceased. " 'F I hed a gun I'd go an' see what kind of a critter 's a-makin' on't," he said, and then half forgot it.

He had come to where he got glimpses of the broad daylight through the palisades of the forest's western border, and where long glints of the westering sun gilded patches of ferns and wood plants and last year's sear leaves, when his quick wood-sight, glancing everywhere and noting everything, fell upon a little bright-colored Indian basket overset in a tuft of ferns, with a few blackberries in it and others spilled beside it. "Why," he said, picking it up and examining it, "that's the baskit I gin' little Polly Pur'n't'n last year! It hain't ben dropped long, for the baries is fresh, 'n' there's a leaf 't ain't wilted scacely. She dropped it, for there's some puckerbaries, an' the' wouldn't nob'dy but a young un pick them. Haow com' that little critter 'way up here?" Then he heard men's voices calling and answering in the woods far away at his left. "God A'mighty, she's lost!" he exclaimed, as he quickly formulated the sounds he heard and the signs he saw. "That was her 'at I hearn! What a dum'd fool I be!" He dropped his bee-box, marking the spot with a glance, and sped back into the heart of the forest so swiftly that the inquisitive chickadees which had gathered about him knew not what way he had gone. He spent no time in looking for traces of the child's passage here, but made his way as rapidly as impossible to the place which the cry had seemed to come from, listening intently as he glided silently along, for he knew that if she had not sunk down exhausted with wandering and fright, she would be circling away after the manner of lost persons, from where he had heard her. Moving more slowly now and scanning every foot of forest floor about him, he at last saw a broken-down stalk of ginseng, its red berries crushed by a footstep, and noting which way it was swept and how recently, found on a bush beyond it a thread of calico, then a small shoe-print in the mould, and farther on a little garter hanging to a broken branch of a fallen tree. According to established usage in such cases, he should have put this in his breast, for he knew that Huldah had knit it, but he only placed it in his pocket, saying, "If she hain't never faound it'll be a sorter comfort tu 'em tu see this—but I'm a-goin' tu find her—I got tu!" He was assured of her course now, and thought she could not be far off, but he did not call, for he knew with what unreasoning terror even men are sometimes crazed when lost in the woods, when familiar sounds as well as familiar scenes are strange and terrible. While for a moment he stood listening he heard the distant halloos of the searching party—then rushing away from them, a sudden swish of leaves and crash of undergrowth, and then caught a glimpse of a wild little form scurrying and tumbling through the green and gray haze of netted shrubs and saplings. He had never stalked a November partridge so stealthily as he went forward now. Not a twig snapped under his foot, nor branch sprung backward with a swish louder than the beat of an owl's wing, and there was no sign in glance or motion that he saw as he passed it, the terror-stricken little face that stared out from a sprangly thicket of mountain yew. Assured that she was within reach, he turned slowly and said softly, "Why, Sis! is this you? Don't ye know me, Sam Lovel? Here's yer little baskit 'at you dropped daown yunder, but I'm afeared the baries is all spilt!" and then he had her sobbing and moaning in his strong arms.

"This is the best day's huntin' ever I done," he said, his voice shaking with the great thankfulness of his heart.

He called again and again to let the searchers know that the lost child was found, but if they heard they did not heed or understand his calls.

When he came to Stony Brook with his burden asleep on his shoulders, he seated her on the bank and bathed her hot face and gave her grateful draughts from a dipper that he made in five minutes with a sheet of birch bark folded and fastened in a cleft stick, and here he shouted lustily again, but got no answer.

"Come, Sis," after listening, stooping and reaching out his arms, "we must be a-moggin' !"

"I be awful heavy, Samwell, but I can't step a step," she said apologetically, as he took her up. "Oh, how good you be !"

Sam's long shadow had ceased following him, and was blurred out in the twilight when he crossed the door-yard chips that his feet had not trodden since that Thanksgiving Day. Polly was asleep again in his arms when he entered the open door of the kitchen which bore a funereal air, with a dozen neighboring women sitting against its walls speaking to each other in hushed solemn voices, one standing beside Mrs. Purington, ready with a hartshorn-bottle when she should take her apron from her face. The poor woman was reaching out blindly with one hand for the comforting salts when Sam, unseen by any till now, set Polly in her lap, and then casting a longing look along the line of gaping, speechless women, he disappeared before the feminine chorus of "Ohs !" and "Mys !" and little shrieks had swelled to its height.

Huldah was out in the back yard trying to comfort herself with listening to the faint halloos of the searchers, and with watching the occasional glimmer of their lanterns and torches, dim stars of hope to her now, when she heard the indoor stir, and hurried in expecting to find her mother in a fainting fit. But there was her little sister with her mother crying over her and scolding her in the same breath, and all the other women letting out their pent-up speech in a hail storm of words, wherewith fell a shower of tears. When she had hugged Polly and kissed her, and sprinkled her with the first tears she had shed that day, she asked, "! Who fetched her?" and out of the confusion got this answer: "Sam Lovel, an' the great good-for-nothin' cleared right aout an' never said one word!"

He could not have gone far. "Samwell! Samwell Lovel!" she called softly, running out toward the road.

"Was you a-callin' me, Huldy?" a low voice answered out of the dusk.

"Won't ye come an' blow the horn tu call 'em hum, Samwell? The' can't none on 'em in there blow nothin'— O *Sam!*"

The tall form of her lover came out of the gloom, and the big sister was in the strong arms that had just brought home the little sister.

The search of the rescue party was prolonged a little before Sam's blasts on the conch-shell were tossed far and wide from echoing mountain to echoing hill to call them home.

"Sam," said Huldah, half an hour later, "you hain't never tol' me whether no you got that 'ere fox?"

"I hain't never hed no chance!" he answered.

XII.

IN THE SHOP AGAIN.

At the next gathering in Lisha's shop, Antoine was present, and when the old cobbler became aware of him, he gave him a hearty welcome, for though he was always cracking rough jokes upon the Frenchman, he had a real liking for him for his good nature and the kindness he had shown at the time of the memorable bear-fight.

"Hello, Ann Twine! Buzzhoo musheer! Cummassy vau! How dy do? Glad t' see ye agin. Oh, you've missed it 't ye hain't ben here t' aour meetin's! Sech stories as the boys has tole, an' Solon Briggs has tole us lots o' things 't we didn't know—nor he nuther."

"Wal naow, Onc' Lasha," asked Antoine in a low voice, as he edged onto the corner of the shoe-bench, "w'at kan o' langwizh dat was, M'sieu Brigg he spik it, hein? 'F dat was Anglish Ah can't nevah larn 'em. He broke ma jaw off. Guess he Sous 'Merican, don't it?"

"Nev' mind, Ann Twine, you c'n onderstand it jes' 's well 's any'on us—'n jes' 's well 's he ken, I guess. It don't hurt us none, 'n' it does him lots o' good to let off them 'ere booktionary words. Wal, Ann Twine, it's your turn naow. You got to tell a story er sing a song. Le's hev Pappy no, come. ' Pappee no sa bum pay-raow.' " Lisha sang with a roaring voice the first line of that once popular Canadian revolutionary song. "'Tune 'er up!"

"Bah Gosh, Onc' Lasha," Antoine said with a sorrowful voice and face, "Ah can' sing, nor tell storee, Ah feel so bad!"

"What's the motter, man? Ye inyuns froze, er terbacker gin aout?"

"No, sah, Onc' Lasha, Ah got plenty onion, plenty tabac, plenty, plenty. But Ah have sush bad dream las' naght! Oh, Ah feel so sorry, me!"

"Tell it, Ann Twine, tell it," Lisha shouted, and all the others joined in the request or demand.

"Ah don' lak tole it, mek you all feel so bad jes' lak me, Ah fred. Wal, don' you cry. Las' naght w'en Ah go bed Ah'll freegit pray. W'en Ah'll git on bed Ah'll tink ov it. Den fus' ting Ah'll say Ah'll shet ma heye, den Ah'll beegin. As' de bon Dieu mek me mo' better as Ah'll was—ef he can—an' tek care hole hwoman an' all the chillens, 'n' mek it heat not quat so much meat, an more patac * and zhonnerkek dat was cheap. Den Ah'll go sleep. Bambye Ah'll dream Ah'll go to l'enfer, what you call it, hell?"

"Guess 't was 'baout mornin' when you dremp that dream, Ann Twine. Mornin' dreams comes true, they say," Lisha put in.

"W'en Ah'll gat dah," continued Antoine, only noticing the interruption by a shrug and a wave of the hand, "de Dev' he come as' me what so good man Ah'll be come dah faw? Ah'll say Ah'll honly come faw fun, see what goin's on, me. Den he say, 'Se' dawn, se' dawn, M'sieu Bissette, mek it youse'f to home.' So Ah'll sit in ver' warm place an' look all 'raoun'. Bambye one

---

* Canuck for potatoes.

hole man come, he don't got any clo's on it, honly jes shoe mek it tool ond' hees arm. Dev' he say, ' What you want it?' Hole man say, ' Dey a'nt have it me on tudder place, so Ah'll come heear, see 'f Ah'll can git it jawb mek it you some boot.' Dev' he stick it aout bose hees foots, one of it lak man's, one of it lak caow's, den he say, ' You can mezzhy only but one of it for mek bose boot; tek it you choose.' Hole man he say, ' Guess Ah'll tek it de bes' foot,' so he mezzhy de man foot an' go work raght off. Pooty soon raght off, bambye, he have it de boot all do, an' Dev' he try it on, an', bah Gosh, de boot fit de caow foot bes', an' he won't go on tudder one 't all, no, sah! Den Dev' he mad, an' keek dat poo' hole man aou' door in col'; an' Ah'll feel so sorree for it Ah'll run raght back here an' git it some clo's, an' tus' one Ah'll git hole of it was Onc' Lasha clo's, an' bah Gosh! you b'lieve it me, dat clo's fit dat hole man jes' if dey been mek it for him, yes, sah!"

The laugh which the relation of this dream aroused was made louder by Lisha's roaring "haw, haw, ho," at the end of which he said, glowering at the narrator through his spectacles, "You dremp that wide awake in the daytime, Ann Twine. You ben studyin' on it up ever sen' you was here?"

"No, sah, Onc' Lasha, Ah'll dream dat in a mawnin'; an' he come true, you say? Wha' you s'pose dat hole man go? Dey won't have it in de good place, dey won't have it in de bad place—wha' you s'pose he goin' go, hein?"

"Guess he'll hafter go t' the 'Hio," Lisha answered, with a laugh that ended in a sigh; " to the 'Hio, where his on'y chick an' child is. Canucks," he continued, "don't never die, 's fur's heard on, 'ceptin' the one 'at I spoke on. When they git old 'nough to die they go to Colchester Pint. Forty, fifty years f'om naow you'll go there, Ann Twine."

"Wal, da't pooty good place to feesh, don't it? Ah'll rudder go dah as come dead."

"Fish! Yes; fish 'n' inyuns 'n' terbacker's baout all a Canuck keers for. Ann Twine, you're the furderest Canuck f'om where ye c'n ketch bull-paouts an' eels 't I ever see. Give 'em them an' inyuns an' terbacker, an' an ole hoss, 'n' a wuthless dog, 'n' they're happy."

"You call it ma dog don't good for somet'ing, Onc' Lasha? You tole him dat he bit you, den he show he good. He fus' rate dog, sah. He lay in haouse all a time honly w'en he barkin' at folks go 'long on road, 'n' he jes' fat as burrer."

"Good qualities, all on 'em," said Lisha, "p'tic'ly in a Canuck dog, bein' as fat 's butter."

"Those 'ere French," Solon Briggs remarked to Pelatiah, who sat beside him, "is a joe-vial an' a fry-volous race."

"Yus," said Pelatiah, sadly regarding the palms of his mittens, much soiled with handling cord-wood since sledding had come, "I s'pose they be pooty smart to run."

Solon, disgusted with his unappreciative listener, raised his voice and addressed the Frenchman. "Antwine, didn't your antsisters come from France?"

"No, M'sieu Brigg, ma aunt seesters an' brudder, too, all bawn in Canada. Ma mudder one of it, seester to ma aunt, prob'ly."

"You misconstrowed my inquirement, Antwine," said Solon. "I meant to ast you, wa'n't their prosperity 'at was borned before 'em natyves of France—reg'lar polly voo Franceys, so tu speak?"

"Ah do' know—yas, Ah guess so, Ah guess yes," Antoine replied at random, having no idea of Solon's meaning.

"Shah! Fur's any conjoogle satisfactualness is consarned, if a man hain't a lingoist he might 's well talk to a sawmill as one o' these furrin Canucks," said Solon, and added, "I b'lieve I'll take my department an' go hum."

"Ah do' know 'f Ah got it raght, zhontemans," said Antoine, as the wooden latch clattered behind the departing wise man, "but Ah tink wat you call Solum in Anglish was dam hole foolish, an't it?" There was not a dissenting voice, but Lisha said apologetically, "Oh, wal, Solon means well!"

"I'll be darned if I know what he does mean," Sam Lovel said.

"Wal," said Lisha, "I s'pose he's a well-read man, an'—"

"Dum the *well* red men!" Sam broke in, "I wish 't they was all sick 'n' dead, consarn 'em! See haow they're cuttin' up aout West 'n' in Floridy!"

"Oh, wall," Lisha continued, "we're well red o' him an' them, so le's don't bother!"

"I don't keer what you say 'baout red men, ef I was a Ninjun as I be a white man," cried Pelatiah, rising and smacking his mittens together, "while 't there was a pale face on the face of the U-nited States of Ameriky, I wouldn't never lay daown my bow-arrers, my tommyhock, an' my wampum: never, no, never!"

"Guess ye'd hev tu lay daown yer wampum 'f I mended yer boots, Peltier," said Lisha, and Sam Lovel advised the budding orator to "save that 'ere fur the spellin' school ex'cises next week."

There was not much further discourse, for Lisha was yawning, and his guests took the hint, as broad as his jaws could compass, and went their ways homeward, Antoine singing "Papineau" at the top of his sonorous voice, and all joining in the ringing refrain, "Hurrah, pour Papineau!" till even the owls were stirred from their solemn propriety, and sent back responsive hoots from their gloomy fastnesses among the steeps of Hogs' Back Mountain.

XIII.

THE FOX HUNT.

A SOFT snow having fallen, not too deep for the comfortable travelling of those so used to such footing as are the hill folks of Northern New England, almost all of Lisha's friends who were wont to gather in his shop had gone fox-hunting.

Many times that day Lisha had stood in the doorway to listen to the voices of the hounds, now wafted softer to his ears from the snow muffled woods than in the brighter days of October, when each hound's note was answered by a dozen echoes, all so sharp and clear that one could hardly tell the real voice from the counterfeit. And once when the music tended toward a runway two furlongs down the road, where the points of two ledges flanked the highway on either side, the old man had taken down his long gun and bare-headed, in his shirt-sleeves, and with his apron flopping about his legs, waddled like a hurried duck half way to the crossing-place. But the fox then changed his course and drew the clamor tapering into silence beyond the crest of a great ridge, and Lisha, after some shivering waiting had cooled his ardor, went back to his bench. He was impatient for evening to come that he might hear how it had fared with the hunters, but they were too leg-weary that night to leave their own firesides, even for the pleasure of "swapping lies" and comparing notes concerning the day's events. The next night, however, brought most of them to the accustomed meeting place, ready to talk or listen. Lisha missed the blonde-bearded face and tall, gaunt form of Sam Lovel, the mightiest hunter of them all.

"Where's Samwill?" he roared, as if he was hailing the mountains. "Them 'ere long laigs o' his'n hain't gin aout, hev they?"

"I sh'd think not," Joe Hill answered; "he went trampoosin' off on 't the North Hill airly this mornin' arter a fox. We hearn the ol' dawg a tootin' on it tu him yit as we come along. 'F Sam c'n git him off he 'll be comin' 'long this way hum tu rights."

"What a darned critter!" said Lisha, his tone expressing more approval than his words, "up an' at it, every day an' all day!"

"Samwell," said Solon Briggs, "is a reg'lar Ramrod, so tu speak; a mighty hunter afore the Lord. He 'll foller a fox from Daniel to Bashaby afore he 'll delinquish the purshoot, or less the nocturnity of night comes on tu him, which that periodical of natur has now arriven an' come, an' therefore he will most proberble du likewise soon."

The sounds of heavy boots being rid of snow by stamping and scraping on the doorstep and the impatient whine of a dog were heard, and the predictions of Joe and the wise Solon were speedily fulfilled by the entrance of Sam and his gaunt, sad-faced hound, with a whiff of chill outer air, as if the hunter had brought down a bagful of the North Hill's breezy atmosphere to sweeten the shop with. As Lisha shouted his welcome the eyes of every one sought first the capacious pockets of Sam's frock, and saw hanging out of one the fluffy brush of a fine fox.

"Wal, Sam, ye got him, hey?"

"Got one on 'em," he said, in a tone that implied no great satisfaction with his luck. "Started two more, but one on 'em holed in half an hour, an' t'other one dodged me till it got so dark I couldn't see tu shoot, 'n' so I called ol' Drive off an' come along."

Drive, who had stretched his weary length by the stove, raised his head and cast a sorrowful look on his master.

"Wal, dawg, ye didn't wanter hunt all night for nothin', did ye?" Sam asked, and Drive, sighing, laid his head again on its pillow of leather scraps, and wagged a few feeble taps on the floor, so signifying that he did not quite understand it, but concluded it was all right.

"Hain't hed a mou'ful t' eat sen mornin', hev ye, Samwill?" Lisha asked, and answered, "Course ye hain't! Mother!" roaring to his wife as if she had been in the next township instead of the next room, and then, as Aunt Jerusha opened the door, "can't ye give Samwill a bite?"

"No, don't gi' me a bite, Aunt Jerushy; I'd ruther you'd gim me a kiss," cried the gallant hunter.

"I sha'n't du nary one, Samwill," said Aunt Jerusha, "I sh'd hev Huldy Purin't'n arter me, but I'll give ye some rye 'n' Injin bread an' col' pork 'n' beans."

"An' give Drive that 'ere hasty puddin'," said Lisha, as Sam and the hound followed Aunt Jerusha into the kitchen. Then Lisha asked, "Wal, boys, haow d'd ye make it a-huntin' yist'd'y. Any on ye kill anythin'?"

"Yes," Joe Hill answered, "Sam killed a fox" ["Of course," said Lisha, in parenthesis], "an' the' was one or two on us got shots at a fox."

"Which Jozeff P. Hill was one," said Solon Briggs, "a-firin' of his gun one several time at two identickle foxes twicte, which opponent du declare the heretobefore-said Jozeff P. did not tu no intense an' puppuses tech ary one on 'em !"

" An' Solon Briggs was another," retorted Joe.

" Nor du I deny the acquisition intire, though my gun discharged an' went off a-pintin' tu a opposyte direction tu what the fox was at them moments of time a occupyin' of, so it can't be said with strict incoherence tu the truth, that I shot at him."

" Haow did that happen ?" Lisha asked.

" Wal, the circumstances was these an' happened thus : I was a-settin' on a lawg a-meditatin' on the mutualability of the human life of mankind, pa'tic'ly in fox-huntin', for I hed n't heard a haoun' in an hour, when my intention was distracted by a leetle noise behind me, an' turnin' my head, there stood a gre't big fox not more 'n three rod off, jes 's if he was an appargotion that had riz aout of the baowels of the airth, which I was flustrated tu the extent of my gun a goin' off an' dischargin' with the butt a-pintin' at the anymil fur cluster 'an what the muzzle was. It was one of the accidentalist accidents that ever happened to my exper'ence, for I hed fust-rate sight on that fox if my gun had only ben pinted right."

" An' what hev you got tu say fur yerself, Jozeff ?"

" Oh, I d' know nothin' what the matter was ailded things," Joe replied, looking up at the low ceiling as if he expected some solution of the cause of his unaccountable misses to come from above. " I guess the ol' gun hain't good for nothin'—or I d' know but the gun 's good 'nough, but the paowder ; I don't b'lieve the paowder 's wuth a darn ! But mebby 't wa'n't the paowder—guess like 's not the shot wa'n't big 'nough, or I spilt some on 'em a-loadin' in a hurry, or suthin' or nuther—I d' know."

"You're sartain 't wa'n't no fault o' your shootin', hain't ye, Jozeff? You shot stret 'nough : we allus du, all on us," said Lisha, his eyes twinkling like the gleam of his awl in the candle-light.

"Wal, I never hed no better sight on nothin' in my life 'n I did on both them 'ere foxes—"

"Not on that 'ere aowl?" Lisha interrupted.

"Humph! We hain't talkin' 'baout aowls! Come to think on 't, I guess they was tew fur off."

"Guess they be naow," from Lisha.

"Wal, anyhaow, I made the fur fly onct!"

"No daoubt on 't, no daoubt on 't, both times, an' jist as fas' as four scairt legs could make it fly! Oh, good airth an' seas! I wish 't I'd got a shot! I'd ha' showed ye! When my old connon gits pinted at 'em, it fetches 'em, I tell ye!"

"Haow clus does it fetch 'em naow, Uncle Lisha?" asked he who never spoke but to propound some great question.

"So clus tu," Lisha answered impressively, "that gen-'ally I can git their skins off on 'em. Peltier," he continued, turning his glasses on the young fellow, "you hain't ben heard from yit."

"Oh, I didn't cal'late tu shoot nothin', only went fer the fun on 't! Didn't see nothin' nor git nothin', only a pocketful o' gum. Hassome?" he asked, passing about his big palm full of spruce gum, like a rudely moulded tray of clay filled with bits of rough amber. Each one took a piece. The smokers laid aside their pipes, the tobacco-chewers resigned their quids, and all went into a committee of the whole to ruminate on the resin of the spruce.

After all the reports were in it was found that none had shot at a fox but Sam, Joe, and Solon, and of these with any success only the first named, who, having now strengthened his interior with a goodly lining of Aunt Jerusha's pork and beans and brown bread, returned to the shop. Declining to exercise his jaw on an offered portion of Pelatiah's treat, he filled and lighted his pipe, and got himself into a restful position on a roll of sole-leather. "Wal," he said, after getting his pipe in full blast, "I seen suthin' on the North Hill 'at's an oncommon sight now-er-days."

"What was that?" one asked, and others guessed "a painter," "a wolf," "a woolyneeg," or the tracks of the animals named.

"Was it the footprints of some avarocious annymill, or the annymill hisself?" Solon Briggs inquired.

"Nary one," said Sam, and added after a few deliberate puffs, during which the curiosity of his auditors grew almost insupportable, "a deer track."

"Good airth an' seas! You don't say so, Samwill? I hain't seen nor hearn tell o' one a-bein' raound in five, I d' know but ten, year. Did ye foller it, Samwill? It's a tol'able good snow fur still-huntin'."

"Foller it? No!" Sam answered emphatically. "What would I foller it for? I wouldn't shoot a deer on these 'ere hills 'f I had a dozen chances at him!"

"I swan I would," said Pelatiah.

"Yas," said Sam, with contemptuous wrath, "you would, I ha' no daoubt on't, an' so would three quarters on 'em shoot the las' deer 'f he come to their stacks an' eat along with their cattle, jes' as Joel Bartlett did, consarn his gizzard! I wish 't was State's prison tu kill a deer any time o' year, an' hed ben twenty year ago. Then we might hev some deer in these 'ere woods, where the' hain't one naow tu ten thousand acres, 'n' where forty year ago the' was hundreds on 'em, 'n' might jes' as well be naow, if 't wan't fer the dum'd hogs an' fools. I knowed critters 'at went on tew legs an' called 'emselves men, 'at when I was a boy useter go aout in Febwary an' March an' murder the poor creeturs in their yards with clubs, twenty on 'em in a day, when they wa'n't wuth skinnin' fur their skins, say nothin' baout the meat, which the' wa'n't 'nough on tew carcasses tu bait a saple trap. An' some o' them things is a-livin' yit, an' would du the same again if they hed the chance. If they was gone an' a wolf left in the place of each one on 'em, the airth would be better off, a darned sight. Cuss 'em, they 're wus 'n Injins!"

The stillness that followed this outburst of the hunter's righteous indignation was broken by Solon's rasping preliminary "Ahem! That 'ere last remark o' yourn is an on-dutible fact. The abregoines would not perforate sech an act, because in so a-duin' they would ampitate their own noses off, deer a-bein' their gret mainstayance, both intarnally an' out-tarnally—that is to say, both food an' remnants."

"Wal," said Lisha, as he soused a tap in his tub, "the' can't nob'dy say 't ever I crusted deer, but the' was 'nough on 'em 't did, twenty, thirty year ago, an' mis'able murderin' business it was, tew. The' was one man, though," he continued, after some vigorous pounding of the tap on his lapstone, "'at got cured o' crustin' for his lifetime, which it shortened it, tew."

"It ort t' been shortened afore ever he went a-crustin'," said the relentless Sam. "Wal, haow was 't, Uncle Lisha?"

"Wal," said Lisha, taking the last peg from between his lips and driving it home, "I guess it's gittin' ruther late t' begin a story t'night, hain't it? Baout what time 's it got tu be, anyway? Peltier, you jes' go t' the kitchen door 'n' ast Jerushy, won't ye?"

"Hol' on; I've got my crow monitor," said Solon, tugging at a leathern thong that hung from his fob, and presently dragging forth what looked like a goodly sized copper porringer, he consulted it for a minute and proclaimed the hour to be "agoin' on tu nine o'clock."

"I want er know! Wal, bein' it's so late, 'n' some on ye 's got quite a piece tu go, I guess I won't tell baout it t'night. Nex' time ye come I will 'f ye 'll put me in mind on 't."

"Prawberbly, in consequent of the demoteness of the inhabitations of some here and present, and the a-proachness of the hour for expirin' to bed, it would be more judiciouser to prefer the narrowation of Uncle Lisha's story ontil another of aour conjovial gatherin's"—which suggestion of Solon's all fell in with, and Sam Lovel, taking his gun from the corner and whistling up his chase-weary hound, all departed, leaving Lisha to snuff out the shop candle and retire to the kitchen, where, smoking the last pipe of the evening with his stockinged feet toasting on the stove hearth, the purring of the cat, the drowsy song of the tea-kettle, and Aunt Jerusha's monotonous counting of the stitches as she narrowed the thumb of a striped mitten, "one — tew — three, narrer; one — tew — three, narrer," soon set him to nodding.

"Why, father," said the good dame, casting a side glance at him from her knitting when his pipe dropped from his mouth, "why don't ye go tu bed, stiddy settin' there a noddin' like a hard's grass head in a July wind?"

"I wa'n't a-noddin' nuther, 'n' hain't a bit sleepy," he said, opening his eyes as wide as possible. "I was on'y medytatin'." But he went to bed.

XIV.

NOAH CHASE'S DEER-HUNTING.

AFTER the soft snowfall the grip of winter tightened with sharper weather, and it was a nipping night when Lisha's friends, the creaking of whose coming footsteps he heard twenty rods away, again entered the shop. Each as he came in made his way quickly to the ruddy, roaring stove, and hardly one failed to shrug his shoulders with a shivering "booh!" rub his hands, stamp his feet, and proclaim in some form of words that the night was cold, as if that was something which needed every man's testimony to establish as a fact.

Joseph Hill remarked, as he rubbed his ears, that "the skeeters bit." The inquirer stared at him, and asked, "Bit who?" and said he hadn't "seen no skeeters sen September."

Another said, "Tell ye what, it's pretty cold," as if he was the original discoverer of this condition of the atmosphere.

Pelatiah asked Sam Lovel, "'S this col' 'nough for ye, Samwel?" and Sam answered, as he fanned himself with his fur cap, "Cold 'nough? No. I want it cold 'nough tu freeze the blaze of a match tu a pipe. I'm most melted,'n' wish 't I could set top o' 'Tater Hill 'n hour er tew 'n' cool off." Pelatiah said, "Sho!" and "guessed he was a-jokin'."

Solon Briggs's opinion was that it was "congealous, and that the muckery would prawberbly condescend to twenty-four below jehu, I wou' say, below zeno, afore mornin'." And Antoine, hugging himself, declared that it was "bien froid," which, after Canuck fashion, he pronounced "ban fret," and then translated, "Col' lak a dev, bah gosh ; more he was Canada, yas, sah." And so encouraging one another, they became firmly settled in the belief that the night was indeed a cold one, and Lisha, as he opened the stove door, using the corner of his apron for a holder, and fed the little demon a bellyful of white birch, gave it as his opinion, that " if the wind riz it would be a reg'lar rip snorter."

"And naow," said Solon, when Lisha had established himself in the polished leathern seat of his bench, " arfter the preluminary remarks 'at you made at aour prevarious meetin', it is confidentially espected 'at you will perceed to dilate your narrowtyve."

"Yas," Antoine urged, "you goin' fill up you promise, don't it, Onc' Lasha, hein ?"

"Wal, boys, 'f I must I must, I s'pose," said Lisha, pulling hard at his pipe between words, " but I hain't no gret at tellin' stories. Ye see"—after some silent back tracking of memory—" 'twas baout Noer Chase ; he was the fust one in taown 't hed a pleasure waggin, 'n' they uster call it Noer's Ark. He'd ben sellick man three fo' years, 'n' sot in the leegislatur' onct—cousin t' Jerushy, tew—'n' orter ben in better business 'n goin' crustin', but he went, 'n' more 'n onct. So one March the' was the alfiredest crust, 'n' he hedn't nothin' tu du much, 'n' says he, ' I guess I'll hassome fun,' says he. So he got him a club, an' put on his snowshoes an' put 'er fer a basin up in the maountin where he knowed the' was some deer a-yardin'. I know the ezack spot, an' so du you, Samwill. Right up where the east branch o' Stunny Brook heads. He got Amos Jones tu go 'long with him, 'n' they got there an' faound the deer, twenty on 'em or more, a-yardin' 'raound in the little spruces, 'n' all poorer 'n wood. Wal, they scahtered 'em aout an' went at 'em. Amos he seen Noer knock down ten on 'em and cut the' thruts, 'n' then he telled 'im for tu stop, f' that was 'nough. But Noer he laughed 'n' said he was jes' beginnin' tu hassome fun ; 'n' then he put arter a doe that was heavy with fa'n, 'n' as he run up 'longside on her, she stumbled in the crust, her laigs all a-bleedin', an' rolled up 'er eyes turrible pitiful tow-wards him, an' gin a beseechin' kind of a blaat. An' Amos he hollered aout tu Noer t' let 'er 'lone, but Noer he on'y laughed 'n' said haow t' he was goin' ter kill tew tu one shot, 'n' he gin 'er a lick on the head with his club 'fore Amos co'ld git tu him."

"Damn 'im !" growled Sam.

"Amos didn't hardly never cuss, but I s'pose he ripped aout then 'n' gin it tu Noer hot 'n' heavy, 'n' said he was a good min' tu sarve 'im 's he'd sarved the doe ; 'n' jes' then he happened tu see that Noer was standin' 'long side o' the doe, right onderneath an onlucky tree, 'n' then he said he knowed suthin' 'ould happen tu 'im, 'n' tol' 'im so. But Noer on'y laughed at 'im, 'n' called 'im a sup'stitious chickin-hearted ol' granny, an' took aout his knife tu cut the doe's thrut. Amos couldn't stan' it tu see no more sech murderin', 'n' so he cleared aout and went hum. Wal, Noer finished the doe, 'n' then took arter a-yullin' buck next. The buck started daown the maountin, 'n' bein' putty light he skinned it 'long putty good jog, so 's 't Noer couldn't ketch up with 'im 's easy 's he hed with t' other ones. So Noer 'gin to git mad, 'n' doubled his jumps, 'n' went tearin' daown hill lickerty split, 'n' hed mos' ketched up tu the deer, when the toe of his snowshoe ketched int' the limb of a blowed-daown tree, an' he fell, kerlummux! 'n' struck his laig on another limb on 't an' broke his laig."

"Good!" cried Sam.

"His laig pained him onmassyfully, 'n' like 'nough he hurt his head tew, for he went inter a swound, I s'pose," continued Lisha, after nodding to Sam, "an' he lay quite a spell 'fore he come tu, 'n' 'twas mos' night. Fust thing, he tried tu git up; but he couldn't make it aout till he got holt of a-saplin' an' pulled hisself up, 'n' then he couldn't take a step. An' while he stood there a-considerin', that 'ere doe appeared right afore him, lookin' at him jes' as she did when he run her daown! He said, 'Shoo!' but she didn't stir a mite, and then he reached daown an' picked up his club an' hove it at 'er, 'n' he said it went through her jes' 's if she'd ben a puff o' smoke, an' it went a-scootin' over the crust twenty rods daown the hill, 'n' she never stirred! He tried to walk agin, but he couldn't step a step, an' then he goddaown on all fours an' crawled 's well 's he could tow-wards the clearin's, an' that ere doe kep' allers jes' so fur ahead on him, allers lookin' at him jes' as she did afore he knocked her in the head. An' when it begin tu grow duskish the' was a wolf set up a-yowlin' behind him as he snailed along a-groanin' an' a-sweatin' like a man a-mowin', an' not goin' more 'n a rod in five minutes, 'n' then tew more wolves jined in a yowlin' so clus tu him 't his toes tickled, 'n' when he looked over his shoulder he could see the dum'd critters a-shoolin' 'long arter him like black shadders, 'n' every naow 'n' then sittin' up on their rumps an' yowlin' for more tu jine 'em. An' all the time that 'ere doe kep' jes' so fur ahead on him, allers a-lookin' at 'im jes' so mournful. Bimebye arter dark, he got tu the clearin', 'n' he couldn't go no furder, so he sot his back agin a tree 'n' sot there an' hollered with his club in his hand, for he'd picked it up in his crawlin', an' there he sot, 'n' there the wolves sot, an' right betwixt 'em stood the doe, which the wolves never took no more noticte on her 'n' of a shadder. Arter a while—seemed 's 'ough 't was a week t' Noer—someb'dy hearn the rumpus, wolves a-yowlin' an' man a-hollerin', an' Aar'n Gove an' Moses Hanson 'n' mongst 'em rallied aout an' went up, an' faound him an' fetched 'im hum. They got a darkter an' sot his laig, but he was sick for three months, 'n' many a time, they said, he seen that 'ere doe a-lookin' in 't the winder 'n' hearn the wolves a-yowlin' raound the haouse, but the' could none o' the rest on 'em see her nor hear the wolves. Bimebye he got better, an' so 's 't he could git aout raound. An' then his son, the on'y one 't he had, went off t' the fur West a-trappin' an' a-tradin' for furs an' skins, an' got killed by Injins, an' then his oldest darter run away with a wuthless, drinkin' goo'-for-nothin' creetur; an' his other darter married an Irishmun, an', wust of all, so Noer said, Amos Jones come up tu see him, and said, 'I tol' yer so!' Then Noer got wus an' run int' the consumption, 'n' arter lingerin' an' lingerin', he died."

"All of which," said Sam Lovel, "sarved him right, and," lifting to his lips the broken-handled pitcher of stale water that stood on a shelf in the corner, seldom replenished but never quite empty, "here's a-hopesin' that all crusters may forever meet the same fate. Amen!"

"Haow long," put in the inquirer, "haow long did Noer Chase hev the consumption?"

"Ten year," Lisha replied.

"Was that all?" said the inquirer.

"I don't b'lieve," said Pelatiah, wiping his nose with his right-hand mitten, "'at ever I'll crust hunt a deer's long 's I live and breathe."

"I don't b'lieve ye will nuther," said Sam, "not in these parts, for ye won't hev the chance. But I wanter tell ye one thing, Peltier, the nex' wust thing tu crustin' deer is snarin' patridges! One day in the fall I was huntin' up through yer father's woods, an' I come acrost a leetle low brush fence with snares sot in the gaps. I tore it all daown, an' one gret cock patridge 't I faound a-hangin' by the neck I hove off int' the woods for the foxes t' eat. You sot them snares, Peltier,'n' you hadn't ort t' done it. Every time I find any sech contraption, I'll spile it, no matter who sot it. 'Xceptin' ugly and mischievous critters 'at won't let ye hunt 'em no ways decent, give all God's creeturs a fair chance. Foller 'em up an' shoot 'em ef ye can, in the times 't they'd ort tu be shot, but not no other times. Not no nestin' good birds nor breedin' an' sucklin' beasts that 's wuth a-savin'. Then when ye die, 'f you've ben honest an' decent tu folks, ye won't hev nothin' tu torment ye. Naow, Peltier, you remember what I tell ye, an' don't ye never snare no more patridges, or less ye 'll hav an ol' hen patridge a-hantin' on ye jes' as that 'ere doe did Noer Chase."

"As true 's I live, Samwill, I won't never again."

"Ez for Noer Chase, which I remember him well as a

consumptuous invalidge in the days of my youthful indolescense," Solon Briggs remarked, " it is my o-pinion that his fate was a just contribution for his predatorious onrightiousness."

" Wal, sah," said Antoine, who had long been waiting to put in a word, " dem Anglish officy in Canada when he go huntin' 'long wid Injin keel moose mos' same like Noel ; fin' 'em in yard, run it daown, shoot it, carree off horn, litly bit meat, skin, maybe, leave it rest of it for wolf. Show horn, ' Hoorah ! Ah keel it moose !' Ah come porty near keel one of dat officy tam Papineau war ; me wish Ah have, bah gosh !"

" I've heard on it, Ann Twine. He chased ye an' you run, an' he follored till he putty nigh broke his wind. He run a narrer chance of his life, sartin."

" Ah, Onc' Lasha, who tole it you dat lies, hein ?"

" I dunno 's I know, Uncle Lisher ; seems 'ogh I did tew, but guess 't I don't," said Joseph Hill, " jes' ezackly what an ' onlucky tree ' is. Dunno but I did know onct, but I've kinder forgot."·

" Wal," said Lisha, " what some calls an onlucky tree, an' thinks is, is a sca'se kind of a tree, half way 'twixt a cat spruce an' a pitch pine. The leaves is longer 'n a spruce 'n' shorter 'n a pine, an' the branches grows scraggider 'n any spruce. They hain't no size—never seen one more'n ten inches 't the butt. They hain't no good, 'n' I d' know 's they be any hurt, but some folks thinks they be, an' you couldn't git 'em tu go a-nigh one for nuthin'. Think if they du the' 'll suthin' drefful happen tu 'em or some o' their folks. I p'sume the' hain't nothin' of it. 'N' naow I guess it's baout time tu shet up shop—an' maouths."

XV.

THE HARD EXPERIENCE OF MR. ABIJAH JARVIS.

The south wind had been roaring for forty-eight hours after its first piercing chill, softening the snow so that it took the imprint of the foot of man and beast as sharp and clear as an impression in wax ; then bringing to its surface weeds and tops of knolls, then making it so splashy that the brooks burst their bonds and overran them in swishing yellow floods, when one January night Lisha's friends came straggling in over the sloppy roads. The talk ran naturally to tracking 'coons, which the weather favored, then to the life and habits of the animal.

"Wal, boys," said Lisha, splashing a tap in the tub, "s'pose ye'll all be arter 'coons termorrer, won't ye? This thaw 'll fetch 'em aout."

"Wal, I d' know," Sam Lovel answered ; "I kind er thought I'd take a little turn arter 'em 'f nothin' happens."

"Dat what we 'll call it chat sauvage in Canada Ah guess so, 'coon ? Dat same ting Ah'll hear it sometam rrrac coon ? Yas ?"

"Sartinly, Antwine," said Solon Briggs, "'coon and raccoon is what we call anonymous terms for one and the same annymill. Raccoon, I expect, is a Latin or Greece word, which 'coon is the English of it."

"Then grease is their name as well as their natur', for they 're the fattest creeturs," said Sam.

"Naow, Antwine," asked Solon, "what might be the true meanin' an' interporation of 'shaw syvadge'?"

"Wall, M'sieu Brigg, lemme see, Ah'll tole you—chat, he mean cat, an' sauvage, he mean he don't tame— m-what you call 'em wil'? Chat sauvage, wil'cat. On'stan'?"

"Hm! yes, wildcat, or tu speak more eggzack, puttin' the cart afore the hoss arter the French fashion, 'cat wild,' similar tu 'shovelnware' for a black hoss, which 'shovel' means hoss an' 'nware' means black. Naow, hain't that a most onnat'ral hist'ry name, so tu speak, for a 'coon or a raccoon, which it hain't noways the natur' of the felime race, but much more resemblances a bear, a-layin' dormouse in winter an' eatin' corn an' shack as much as meat victuals, as no critters of the cat speshy do?"

"Sartin, Solon, you're right," said Sam, "a 'coon 'ould make a first-rate little bear 'f 'twan't fer his tail. He's jes' as independent, an' hoggish, an' sorter cunnin'-foolish, an' fond of water an' mud, an' sweet-toothed, an' hot-toothed, tew, fer he'll dig wild turnips an' eat 'em jes' 's a bear will. Haow on airth any critter 't ha'n't got its maouth an' insides lined with sheet iron can chaw an' swaller a green wild turnip 's more 'n I can understand. Why, it's wus 'n forty thaousan' red-hot needles a-jabbin' int' yer tongue, 'f ye ever bit one."

Almost every one present confessed to having been fooled in the days of his youth by some rough practical joker into tasting the bulbous root of the plant, whose snake-like spathe should warn one that it biteth even like a serpent and stingeth like an adder.

"Wal, naow," said Lisha, laying aside his lapstone, shoving his spectacles on to the top of his head, and resting his elbows on his knees, "that makes me think of a man 'at I knowed 'at come tu his death along o' foolin' a boy with a wild turnip, 'n' I d' know but what it sarved him putty nigh right, naow ra'ly I don't. His name was Bijer Jarvis. Why, some on ye knowed 'im; he use ter run the sawmill up in the Notch. He was a red-headed, cross-grained, ill-natured creetur, 't would druther see folks in hot water 'n aout on 't. Good airth an' seas! 'f I ha'n't spoke in meetin', fer he was Peltier's uncle! Peltier's mother was a Jarvis. But she wa'n't tu blame fer it, 'n' I hain't goin' tu spile a story fer relation's sake, so ye need n't take no pride in what I say, Peltier."

"Honh! Gol darn Uncle Bije! Blast his ole picter!" exclaimed Pelatiah, "he never done nothin' fer none o' aour folks ony cheat father aout 'n a yoke o' tew-ye'r-ol' steers, so I hearn 'em tell. Ye need n't spile no stories baout him on my 'caount, Uncle Lisher."

"Wal," Lisha continued after this little interruption, "Bijer was a-runnin' the sawmill, an' one mornin' when he was a-goin' 'long the road through the woods tu the mill he seen a wild turnip an' pulled it, an' kerried it 'long, thinkin' mebbe 't he'd dry it agin he had a cough in the fall, for some sets gret store by wild turnips dried an' grated an' took in 'lasses fer a hackin' cough. Curous, hain't it, 't when they're dried they ha' no more taste intu 'em 'n a piece o' chalk? Wal, he mogged along tu the mill an' rolled a lawg on t' the kerridge an' dogged it an' histed the gate, an' jes' then there come along a boy a-fishin' o' the name o' Morrison, an' stopped tu see him saw. He was al'ays a-gawpin' raound, lookin' at the contraptions an' askin' questions, more 'n boy-fashion, fer he seem tu be kinder studyin' intu 'em, 'n' they said 't he made a reg'lar little sawmill complete, kerridge, rag wheel an' all, an' sot it a-runnin' in a brook clus tu his folkses. It al'ays made Bijer crosser 'n two sticks tu see him raound, 'n' he didn't take no notice on him till bimeby he happened tu think of the turnip, 'n' he ast 'im 'f he liked apples, 'n' he said he did, fer who ever see a boy 't didn't? Then s' he, ' Did ye ever eat any sweet graound apples? Here's one o' the sweetest ever ye see,' handin' on 'im the turnip; ' take a bite o' it.' The boy took a good bite an' chawed it kinder slow, lookin' at Bijer, but Bijer looked turrible honest 'n' clever 's he ever could, so the boy didn't think nothin'. In tew three minutes it begin tu take holt, 'n' then he begin tu sputter 'n' spit 'n' cry, an' holler 't his maouth was full o' bumble-bees an' hornets, 'n' Bijer settin' there on the lawg goin' intu fits a-laughin' at 'im, till the boy cleared aout, mos' crazy with the fire in his maouth, 'n' Bijer didn't see nothin' on 'im agin fer a month, till one day he popped up ahind a pile o' boards a-shakin' his fist at 'im an' hollered, ' You ol' red-headed heap ! I'll pay ye some time, see 'f I don't, 'n' scooted aout o' sight 'fore Bijer could fling an aidgin' at 'im. All this while an' arter, things kep' gittin' aout o' kilter raound the mill : sticks in the wheel, bull-wheel rope wore aout 'n' breakin', saw duller 'n a hoe, all kinder onaccaountable, nobody knowed haow. Bimeby long late in the fall when the pond froze over, Bijer was a-fussin' raound the bulkhead one day, choppin' a lawg loose, or suthin' nuther, 'n' bimeby he broke through an' went in kersouze ! 'n' he couldn't git aout, fer the ice wouldn't hold an' the lawgs an' bulkhead 'n' things was all ice, so 's 't he couldn't keep no holt on 'em, 'n' the water all the while a-suckin' his laigs int' the flume. Jest then he seen that 'ere boy come skatin' 'long the pond, 'n' he hollered fer him tu reach him a pole or a board, but the boy kep' a skitterin' raound a-laughin' at 'im, an' says he, ' Ole red-head, don't ye wish 't ye hed one o' them sweet graound apples tu warm ye up ? Mus' be kinder cool bathin' in there. I'd go 'n' dig ye one 'f 't wa'n't all froze up.' Bijer begged an' cussed an' sploshed raound, an' cussed an' begged, 'n' last when he was mos' tuckered aout he begin tu pray, 'n' then that 'ere imp of a boy hooked a pike pole into his cut-collar an' hauled him on t' the ice 'n' snaked him ashore. He couldn't stan', 'n' the boy went arter somebody, 'n' they kerried 'im hum. He never got well agin arter, nor able tu walk. Some said 't was rheumatiz, 'n' some said 't was dyspepsy in the laigs—I do' know. One day the nex' summer when they'd sot 'im aout on the stoop tipped back in his cheer, that 'ere darned boy come along 'n' stood 'n' gawped at 'im. Bimeby says he, ' Mr. Jarvis,' says he, ' I've brung ye suthin' 't 'll du ye good. I've took lots o' trouble tu git it for ye.' 'N' he pulled an alfired gret wild turnip rut aout'n his pocket. ' Take a bite an' chaw it daown,' says he, a shovin' on it under his nose ; ' take a bite ; I've owed ye one more'n a year.' Bijer gin a kinder start, 'n' the hind laigs of his cheer slipped, 'n' he come daown ker lummux ! 'n' hurt his head some way so 's 't he died in a week or tew. 'N' that's what *he* got for feedin' boys wild turnips.''

" Bah gosh ! Ah guess wen he begin to dead he'll sorry he foolish dat boys, an't it ?''

" That boy," said Solon, " was vindictative."

" I do' know as that was what they called it," said Lisha ; "seems though they said he was injinnew-ous.

Anyway, he went off, 'n' they say 't he's what they call a injin-near on one o' them 'ere steam railroads daown in Massachusetts somewheres."

"Du you think, Sammywell," Solon asked, getting back to the subject under consideration, "that the vocal voice of a 'coon resemblances a screechaowl?"

"Wal," Sam answered, "I do' know. Some says that a 'coon does make a noise sometimes 'at saounds suthin' like a screechaowl, only kinder hoarser. I had a tame 'coon onct fer most a year, but I never hearn him du anything but graowl when he was mad, an' squall when he was hurt, jes' you've hearn' em when a dawg hed a holt on 'em. He was the cunninest little cuss! Intu all the mischief he could think on, an' more tew. The chickins hed tu suffer when he got intu the hen haouse, every time, 'n' he'd raise tunkit with everything he could git intu in the haouse. When he was eatin' he'd keep a-sozzlin' his grub in his pan o' water all the time. Uncle Lisher makes me think on 'im every time he sploshes his luther in his tub. Shouldn't wonder, Uncle Lisher, 'f you turned intu a 'coon yit."

"Darn'd 'f I wouldn't like tu part o' the year, Samwill. Wouldn't it be cute to curl up when the col' weather come on an' snooze till spring or a thaw come, an' not haf tu bother gittin' wood or grub?"

"Ye'd want tu take yer long pipe with ye, an' some terbacker an' matches in yer pocket when ye went intu a holler tree—'t would be lonesome goin' without a smoke so long."

"Naow, does 'coons hev pockets?" asked the man who never spoke but to ask a question.

"Course they du," Sam answered shortly; "inside

pockets, 'n' I d' know but cut-tail pockets an' trowses pockets. An' then agin, Uncle Lisher, when the' come a thaw an' ye turned aout an' went traipsin' raound an' somebody tracked ye intu another tree, haow 'd ye like tu hev 'em cud daown the tree 'n' knock ye in the head?"

"'T would be you, Samwill, 'at faound me, an' you'd know me by the smell o' luther, 'n' you wouldn't hurt yer Uncle Lisher. 'N' I'm glad you made me think on 't, fer I guess I'd ort tu hev a smuk afore I turn intu a 'coon." Whereupon he cleaned the bowl of his pipe with an awl, ran a waxed end through the stem, blew through it, and then shaving some tobacco from a plug on his cutting-board with a shoe-knife, was presently in the full enjoyment of what he called a "ri'daown good smuk."

"Ah bet too he a'n't fregit when he be 'coon as' you, Sam, haow you lak it you boot, an' when you tole 'im he too tight he say ' he straysh!' Wen you tole 'im he too loose, he say 'he shrimp!' Hein, Onc' Lasha, you don't fregit dat, a'n't it?"

"Arrrh! You dum peasouper!" Lisha growled, like a good-natured bear.

"'F you want fur," said Sam, "trackin' 'coons on the snow 's all well 'nough, but it's mortal hard work wallerin' in the soft snow all day. But 'f you want fun an' music, take yer dawgs an' hunt 'em nights in cornfiel's, an' where they've ben shackin' under sweet acorn trees, an' sometimes you'll strike a track 'long a brook where they've ben a-froggin'. Hev tew three good haoun's a-hootin' on a track fer a good spell, an' then singin' halleluyer raound a tree! That's what I call fun alive! Some druther hev a cur dawg 'at won't bark till he trees, but gimme more music, 'f I've got tu hev less 'coons."

"Wal," said Lisha, ramming his pipe with the handle of his awl, "everybody tu their notion, 's the ol' woman said when she kissed her kyow, but I could n't never—sen' I was a boy—see no gret fun in stumblin' raound in the dark 'n' fightin' skeeters half the night, fer one or tew 'coons with baout as much hair on 'em 's the' is on the back o' yer hand, 'n' like 's not, not git nary 'coon arter all."

"Why, Uncle Lisher," said Sam Lovel, "didn't we hev fun the night the 'coons broke up the school-meetin'?. an' is that ra'ly your idee of the fun o' huntin', jest tu git suthin' that's wuth money? Seems tu me, if fur an' meat 's all a feller 's arter, he ain't goin' tu git no gret comfort aout on 't."

"Shaw, Samwill! you hain't a-goin' tu ondertake tu make me b'lieve 't you don't feel better a-bringin' hum a fox skin, er a 'coon skin, er half a dozen patridges, 'n' ye du comin' hum wi' nothin'? I know better 'n' that."

"Of course I like tu git suthin' tu show fer a day's hunt, an' it's comf'table tu the feelin's tu make a good shot, but 'f I didn't never git nuthin' only what I c'n show, I sh'ld stay tu hum more 'n what I du. If dollars an' cents an' suthin' t' eat was all I was arter, I'd snare patridges 'n' trap foxes, an' you never heard o' my doin' nary one."

"Wal, then, Samwill, what on airth du ye go fer? Ye hunt more 'n' 'most anybody I know, an' ye git more game."

"I can't hardly tell, Uncle Lisher. It comes nat'ral fer me tu run in the woods. 'F I du git more game tu show for it 'n' some does, I git suthin' besides 't I can't show. The air o' the woods tastes good tu me, fer 't hain't ben breathed by nothin' but wild creeturs, 's 'n ole feller said 'at useter git up airly daown in Rho'dislan', where my folks come from. I luffter breathe it 'fore common folks has. The smell o' the woods smells good tu me, dead leaves 'n' spruce boughs, 'n' rotten wood, 'n' it don't hurt it none if it's spiced up a leetle bit with skunk an' mink an' weasel an' fox p'fum'ry. An' I luffter see trees 'at 's older 'n any men, an' graound 't wa'n't never plaowed 'er hoed, a-growin' nat'ral crops. 'N' I luffter hear the stillness of the woods, fer 't *is* still there. Wind a-sythin', leaves a-rustlin', brooks a-runnin', birds a-singin', even a bluejay a squallin', hain't noises. It takes folks an' waggins an' horses an' cattle an' pigs an' sech to make a noise. I git lots o' things a huntin' 't I can't show ye nor tell ye baout, an' a feller that don't, don't git the best o' huntin', 'cordin' to my idee.''

"I do' know but what ye've got baout the right on 't, Samwill," said Lisha, after smoking slowly and gazing for some minutes out into the dark through his long window, "I do' know but what ye hev, Samwill. Wal, boys, 'f ye 'r goin' arter 'coons termorrer ye'll want'er sleep some fust." And he arose and took off his apron, and presently the wooden latch clicked behind the last departing guest.

XVI.

THE COON HUNT.

One February night when the crusted snow on the ridges and drifts shone brighter than burnished silver in the slanting rays of the newly-risen moon, Lisha's friends arriving in force found the old man studying his almanac by the light of his little candle. So absorbed was he in the latest work of his favorite author that he barely noticed the entrance of his visitors, and only gave one comprehensive nod of general recognition and welcome, without averting his gaze from the limp little pamphlet, already well worn, though not yet two months off the store-keeper's shelf.

"Be you a-studyin' of the prognostifications of the weather, Uncle Lisher?" Solon Briggs inquired, craning his neck sidewise from his seat by the stove, "or be you merely divertin' the intellecks of your mental mind, a perugin' of the antidotes? I b'lieve," he continued, addressing the company generally, after waiting in vain for an answer, "'at the' is more solider inflamation and stay-tistics in the V'mont Re-*gis*ser 'an what the' is in Middlebrookses' Farmer's Almynack, which Uncle Lisher is a-readin' of; but Middlebrookses' is tol'able hefty on weather productions, drawin' aside the screenins o' futur' comin' events, as it ware, an' the antidotes an' re-cypes is amusin' an' instructin'. I see 'at the' 's tew re-cypes fer curin' hams.

Like 'nough Lisher 's studyin' them, bein' 'at he killed a hawg last week."

But Uncle Lisha's spectacles were brought to bear on the page headed with the gray wood-cut of two men breaking and swingling flax, and in the background a prancing horse hitched to a sleigh that he never could break was being swingled by his driver with a club of a whip. Lisha's forefinger went down the columns of the days of the weeks and month as slowly as ran the cautious weather prophecy:

```
....................... ....Now expect
....................... ....cold weather
........  .................and good
....................... ....sleighing for
............................. ....some
(Sexeg. Sunday)................time
(☉ low in South.)
...........................Cloudy
.........  ..........cold weather and
.................................likely
..............................for snow,
.................................rain
....................................and
..................................hail.
.........  ............. High winds
............................and
(G. Washington b. 1732.)
...............................cold.
...........................  ..Snow.
```

till it stopped at "26, Sat.," and underscored the date with a deep nail-mark. "Good airth an' seas!" he shouted. "Boys, did ye know 't this was the twenty-sixt' of Febewary? This is the day 't the ol' bear comes aout! He's seen his shadder, 'n' he won't poke his nose int' the daylight agin fer forty days. We sh'll hev' a col' March, 'n' like 'nough the wind 'll be north when the sun crosses the line, 'n' then we'll hev' a back'ard spring 'n' a poor corn year."

"Bah gosh! Onc' Lasha, ef dat de way you goin' mek wedder, Ah ant want it you mek heem for me more as a week! Dat way you'll ant rose no corn fo' you bear, hein?"

"Arghem!" Solon Briggs began, clearing his throat and sticking his thumbs in the arm-holes of his vest, "I hev my daoubts consarnin' the paower of human mortality tu foretell the comin' futur' weather, which it bein' the case, it hain't no way phillysophycable that beasts an' annymills, which human man is sot above 'em, has that segashiousness gin 'em. Haow is wild geese a-goin' tu know more 'n we du when winter's a-comin', or mushrats tu perpare their inhabitations—when they build haousen—fer a more 'n oncommonly tough winter, or bears an' woo'chucks know whether the spring 'll be back'ard or for'ad? Haowever notwithstandin', I du not deny there bein' signs gi'n whereby an' by which we can tell suthin' more or less haow the weather's a-goin' tu be, sech f'r instance as hawg's melt an' the hus's o' corn, the haighth o' weeds an' et cetery."

"Wal, Solon," said Sam, "your idees an' mine don't jibe egzackly. You 'low 't a man can tell if it's goin' tu be a hard or open winter by lookin' 't a hawg's melt 'n' corn hus's an' so on—but annymills can't tell by nothin'. Naow, I don't b'lieve there's any tellin' by a hawg's melt nor corn hus's, fer you'll find dif'fent shaped melts in dif'fent hawgs killed the same day—an' what awdds does 't make tu an ear o' corn whether the hus's is thick or thin 's long 's they'll be loosened off 'fore winter anyway? An' the weeds grows tall 'cause it's a-growin' season, not 'cause the snow 's goin' tu be deep. But 'sposen a man can tell by signs 't he sees. Why can't annymills, 'at can see things, an' hear things, an' smell things 't we can't begin tu? A turkey 'll see a hen hawk 'fore it begins tu be a speck in the sky tu you an' me, an' by seein' or smellin' a crow 'll find carri'n milds off; a fox 'll smell a maouse, or hear him squeak or rustle the grass furder 'n we c'ld see one on the snow, an' he can smell the tech o' yer finger on a bait fer a week arter. Swallers know when it's goin' tu rain or blow. Mebby they can smell weather—I d' know. An' dumb creeturs has got senses 't we ha'n't got, besides hevin' aourn a good deal sharper 'n we hev. Haow does a haoun' dog strike a bee-line fer hum when he's done a-huntin', or a cat 'at's ben kerried in a bag thre mild find her way back, or birds find their way thaousan's o' miles back an' tew year arter year, or foxes know runways 't they never seen? Fer my part, I'd a good deal druther trust tu dumb creeturs foretellin' the weather 'n seasons 'n I would tu what I c'ld find aout by studyin' melts an' hus's. I'd druther take a wild goose's or a mushrat's actions 'an I would even your word for 't, Solon."

"You can b'lieve what y'r min' tu, Sammywell, but I b'lieve 'at there is sartin signs gi'n fer aour guidancin', which, f'r instance, I wouldn't kill my hawgs or my beef-crutter in the old o' the moon onless I wanted the meat tu shrink in the cookin', ner sow my peas in the wanin' o' that lunimary 'f I wanted 'em tu grow luxuberant."

"Wal, wal, boys," said Lisha, who had hung the almanac on its nail by the window and got some work in hand, " nev' mind baout the signs, an' ' nev' mind the weather when the wind don't blow.' I'm achin' to hear what luck ye hed arter 'coons that day. I hearn 't ye most all went."

" Ast Joe," some one said, and Lisha asked, glaring at Joe between his shaggy eyebrows and the top of his spectacles. " Haow is 't, Jozeff? Be you cock o' the walk this time?"

" Wal, I d' know but what I be, 'f ye caount walkin' an' choppin'. I da' say I done 's much o' that 's any on 'em. I 'spose 'f I don't give a full 'caount on 't, some on 'em 'll give a fuller one. Wal, I went, an' Peltier he went along with me, 'n' he didn't kerry no axę; said 't he'd got a lame shoulder 'n' couldn't chop 'thaout mos' killin' on 'im. It got well tu rights, though, fer I seen 'im choppin' cord wood nex' day. We started aout baout eight 'clock er ha'-past—mebby 't wa'n't more 'n eight—I d' know, quarter arter, mebby, 'n' struck a track where three 'coons 'd ben 'long daown in the Beav' Medder swamp in the night. The tracks went a-saunderin' raound hither an' yon, 'n' fin'ly went off up on 't the hill east, 'n' then north—no 't wa'n't, 't was saouth— 'n' then east agin 'n' then north 'n' then east, an' says I to Peltier, says I, they've went int' the laidges 'n' 't a' no use in us follerin' on 'em; but Peltier, says he, le's us foller 'n' see where they hev gone. Like 'nough we c'n trap 'm aout. So we follered an' follered, snow knee deep, till bimeby, arter they'd went all raound Robin Hood's barn, they went towward the Beav' Medder agin, an' into 't, an' stopped t' the all-tummuttablest gret big ellum in the hull swamp—the tracks did. We searched all raound, 'n' couldn't find 't they'd went any furder, 'n' so I off wi' my cut an' begin tu chop. An' I chopped an' chopped, 'n' Peltier he stood raound encouragin' on me 'n' chawin' gum an' gruntin'—every time I swatted the ol' axe int' the tree, he'd grunt—I tell ye, he grunted like a good feller, 'nough tu chop a cord 'n' a half o' wood. That ere ol' ellum was jes' 's solid as ol' pork clean tu the middle, 'n' 'twas all o' three foot through, I d' know but three foot 'n' a half—mebby 't wa'n't but three foot through—anyway, 't was tougher 'n' a biled aowl, 'n' the' wa'n't no holler in the butt, 'n' I tol' Peltier, I did, 'at I'd bate a cookey the' wa'n't a dum 'coon in the pleggid ol' ellum. Wal, I chopped an' chopped, till I sweat like a man a-mowin', an' I tell ye I was glad when I see the ol' tree begin tu tottle an' then come daown kersmash! An' I'll be dum'ed if it didn't lodge in another ellum half as big! An' I hed to chop that daown tew, Peltier helpin' on me, chawin' gum an'gruntin'. Wal, sir, when we got it cud daown, baout noon I guess 't was—mebby arter—mebby not more'n ha' past 'leven—the' was a hole most 't the top big 'nough tu hold a dozen 'coons, an' the' wa'n't a dum'ed one in it! It hed froze jest a leetle towward mornin', 'n' they'd come aout an' gone off on the crust. But we hed us a heap o' fun, didn't we, Peltier?"

"Honh!" Pelatiah snorted, "I do' know but what you did."

"Wal, Samwill," said Lisha, "it's your turn naow."

"Oh, I didn't du nuthin' much. Follered tew int' an old basswood stubb 't I could mos' push over, an' got them an' one 't was in there afore."

"Julluk your luck, Samwill," said Lisha.

"I faound a cur'us kind of a thing in the stub, sort of

a 'coon plaything, I reckon it is. I brung it along tu show ye," said Sam, taking out of his pocket a knot or gnarl about the size of a man's fist, and worn quite smooth with much handling (or footing) by the raccoons.

"Wal," said Lisha, after this had been passed around and examined by all, Pelatiah chipping a side of it with his knife and smelling it, "Wal, wha' 'd you du, Solon?"

"I did not precipitate in the sports and aversions of the day."

"Onc' Lasha, what for you ant ask it me?" cried Antoine. "Bah gosh! 'f Ah'll git all a 'coon what Ah'll see dat tam, Ah'll tole so big story you mos' can' b'lieve him, sah."

"Wal, Ann Twine, 'sposen you tell us what ye seen. I ha' no daoubt that 'll be all 't we c'n swaller tu onct."

"Wal, sah, Ah 'm 's go'n' tole you de trute, jes' sem always Ah do. Ah'll go 'lone, 'cause all what Ah git Ah want heem masef, jes' lak Sam, ant it, Sam? Ef t'ant for dat Ah'll have it somebody for what you call heem—m—wisnit? Fus ting Ah say, Ah'll want you rembler Ah don't goin' tole you where Ah see what Ah'll see' 'cause Ah 'm 's goin' git it some tam, me.

"Wal, sah, Ah go fin' track one chat sauvage, folla him leetly way Ah fin' nudder come wid it, bamby nudder, den nudder, den nudder. Ah see so much track Ah mos' can' co'nt it—ten, fifteen, twentee, prob'ly more as tree four tree full Ah guess so. Wal, Ah folla, folla, folla ver' long way. Bamby Ah hear it nowse, mos' lak big hammer ov' dar in de forge, ony he ant go so fas'—*Boom! Boom!*—so, 'baout fas' you breeze you bress. More furder Ah go, more was be dat nowse louder, an Ah begin mos' be 'fred, me, but Ah don' care, Ah'll folla dem track till

Ah come close to big laidge, an' dat track all go in leetly hole jes' mos' too small 'nough for one 'coon sauvage. Den Ah see what mek it dat nowse. *Yes*, sah, you b'lieve it me, de whole top dat laidge, big, big rock, more bigger dis shawp, he lif' up 'baout two ninches *ver-y* slow— so—den come daown *boom !* den lif' up, den come daown *boom !* Bamby Ah'll hear it more leetly nowse when rock lif' up—*Squon-n-n-h !* lak Onc' Lasha mek it when he be sleep, ony not so louder lak Onc' Lasha. Bamby putty soon Ah bee-gin be not so 'fred, an' den Ah'll peeck in hole. Evry tam rock lif' up lit shine in so Ah can see; an' what you tink Ah see? More as tree—honded— tausen chat r-r-raccoon—all fas' sleep ! Yes, sah ! Evry tam he pull his bref he swell up full of breeze an lif' up rock. Wen he let it go his bref, den rock come daown— *boom !* Ah'll see it; he so far in off Ah can' git it. No, *sah*, Ah ant gat not one *of* it ! Das *too* bad. Oh, *too* bad, too bad !"

"Wal, I swan tu man !" said Solon, exhaling a long breath. "I du declar, Antwine, you're wus 'n Annymias an' Sophier fer onvoracity."

"I move," said Lisha, pitching away his hammer and tumbling his lapstone on to the floor, "I move 'at this 'ere meetin' du a journ afore it gits so mad 'at it up an' kills that 'ere dum'ed 'tarnal lyin' Canuck ! An' I secont the motion an' it's kerried unamous."

"Du you ra-ly 'spose," the questioner whispered in Joseph Hill's ear as they went out into the moonlight, " 'at Antwine *was* a lyin' ?"

XVII.

IN THE SUGAR CAMP.

The first warm days of spring had come, when for all the chill of the frosty nights, the sky and the white clouds drifting across it looked soft and hazy as in summer. The voice of the crow had become a familiar sound again ; the first robin had been reported ; more than one bluebird had sung its short sweet song in the valley ; and Lisha had seen a phebe perched on a dry sunflower stalk in his garden, and making thence her unerring swoops upon the flies that, thawed to life again, buzzed about the sunny side of the fence. The snow was deep in the woods yet, but it had grown coarse grained, and all the winter litter of branches and twigs and latest fallen leaves seemed to be upon its surface, and it was gray in patches with myriads of ever-moving snow fleas. In the open whole southward-sloping fields were bare and brown except their borders of drifts, and here and there bits of the road were dry and firm, most pleasant to feet long accustomed to the uncertain and slippery footing of wintry ways. Here and there at a homestead a man or boy in shirt-sleeves was working up the great pile of sled-length wood into fuel, but most of the " men folks" were away in the sap works gathering their great harvest of the year.

Among the tall maples that grew on some hillside of every farm the smoke of the sugar camp drifted upward, and the daily and nightly labors there of all Lisha's friends had for some time prevented their customary visits to the shop. Lisha having, as he said, "got tew ol' an' short-winded tu waller raound in the snow, an' never could git the heng o' snow-shoein'," had hired Pelatiah to do his sugar-making, while he attended to his shoemaking and mending. But getting very lonely with his solitary labors, during a slack run of sap he sent his henchman out among his friends with a verbal "invite" to a sugaring off at his camp on a certain evening. Accordingly at "airly candle-ligh'in'," the guests came straggling in, and were loudly and warmly welcomed by their host. "I'm dreffle glad tu see ye, boys! I hain't sot eyes on ye fer a month o' Sundays, seems 'ough. Make yerselves tu hum, an' I'll sweeten ye up tu rights." The little open-fronted shanty faced a rude fireplace, a low wall of rough stones enclosing on three sides a square yard wherein burned a rousing fire that shed a comfortable warmth into the farthest corner of the shanty, and lighted up the trees for rods about. To one side stood the "store trough," a huge log hollowed out to hold the sap as gathered. The great potash kettle slung by a log-chain to its monstrous crane, a tree trunk balanced on a stump, was swung off the fire, and the syrup was bubbling in a smaller kettle, carefully tended by Lisha and Pelatiah.

"Wal, boys," the old man said, after testing the syrup for the twentieth time by pouring it slowly out of his dipper, "it begins tu luther-ap'n, an' I guess it's baout ready. Peltier, you put aout an' git tew three buckets o' clean snow; Samwill, ketch a holt o' that 'ere stick an' help me histe this 'ere kittle off. Naow, then, fetch up some seats, the' is sap tubs 'nough layin' raound. Samwill, Jozeff, Solon, some o' ye, the' 's a baskit of biscuit in back there under my cut, an' a bowl o' pickles; won't ye jes' fetch 'em aout?"

So bustling about, he at last got his guests seated around the kettle of hot sugar and the buckets of snow, and they fell to, each in turn dipping out some syrup, and pouring it in dabs upon the snow, when it presently cooled into waxy clots ready for eating.

"Pass raound them 'ere biscuits, Peltier—ta' keer, don't tip the kittle over wi' yer dum'ed hommils! Mos' 's good 's wild honey, hain't it, Samwill?" Lisha asked, smacking his lips after disposing of a big mouthful.

"I d' know but what it's jist as good t' eat," said Sam, "but the' hain't much fun a-gittin' on it."

"Naow, du you r'aly think the' is much fun in bee-huntin', Samwill?" Lisha asked.

"Sartinly I du. 'Tain't so excitin' as fox-huntin' an' sech, but it takes a feller int' the woods in a pleasant time o' year, an' it's interestin' seein' the bees a-workin' an' seein' haow clust you c'n line 'em and cross-line 'em, an' a feller's got tu hev' some gumption, an'—wal, I'd a good deal druther hunt bees 'an tu lug sap."

"By gol! so 'ld I," said Pelatiah. "My shoulders is nigh abaout numb kerryin' the gosh darned ol' neck-yoke."

"It mus' be tough on that 'ere lame shoulder o' yourn, Peltier," Joe Hill remarked, withholding a paddleful of sugar from his open jaws, while he bestowed a general wink upon the party.

"Honh! I hain't got no lame shoulder in p'tic'lar—not naow, I hain't."

"Wal naow, boys," Lisha said, after all had plied their

paddles silently but diligently for some time, "this is what I call bein' kinder sosherble agin. 'Tain't quite so cosey as the shop, but we've got all aou'doors for room"

"Not inside on us, we hain't—leastways I hain't"—said Joe Hill; "this 'ere maple sweet is turrible fillin'."

"Take a pickle if y'r cl'yed, Jozeff, an' begin agin," Lisha urged, on hospitable deeds intent, but Joe declined, and soon all but Pelatiah desisted and tossed into the fire the little wooden paddles which had served as spoons.

"This is what I call raal comfort," said Sam Lovel, after lighting his pipe with a coal and stretching himself on the evergreen twigs in the shanty. "The' hain't nothin' like an aou'door fire an' a shanty like this an' a bed o' browse fer raal genywine restin' comfort!"

"Wal, it hain't bad for onct 'n a while in pleasant weather; but fer a steady thing, I'd a leetle druther hev a good ruff over my head, an' plarstered walls raound me, an' a fireplace or a stove," said Lisha, and then to avoid unprofitable discussion—"Samwill, I s'pose ye don't git much huntin' naowadays. Tew late fer huntin' foxes an' tew much bare graound fer trackin' 'coons. Git a patridge onct 'n a while, though, I s'pose, don't ye?"

"No, sir," said Sam, with emphasis; "haint't shot a patridge in a month. I want the' should be some next year. I killed a fisher, though, t'other day."

"I wanter know! Shoot him? 'Tain't often 't a feller gits a chance tu shoot one o' them critters. Awfle hard tu git a shot at, they be, I s'pose?"

"Yes, and hard tu kill when ye du git a shot at 'em. Drive treed this one, an' he went a-skivin' through the tree-tops baout as spry 's a squirrel. I let 'im hev it on the run—hed in buckshot an' three Bs—an' disenabled him so 's 't he couldn't jump; but I hed tu shoot him twict more 'fore he come daown, an' then hommered his head a spell 'fore he'd quit a kickin'. Then I tied his hind laigs together an' slung him on my back an' started fer hum."

"Wha'd ye wanter lug his carkiss for? Why didn't ye skin 'im?"

"Oh! I—ah," said Sam, stammering and blushing, "I wanted tu show him tu—tu—some o' my folks 'at hedn't never seen the hull critter; nothin' but the skins."

"H-m. Some o' my folkses' names begins with H-u-l d-y P-u-r—"

"'N' 's I was a-tellin' on ye," Sam broke in hurriedly, "I hed him on my shoulder slung ont' my gun berril, an' hed kerried him much 's half a mild, an' goin' 'long through some little thick secont growth, suthin' ketched an' most pulled the gun off 'm my shoulder, and I'll be shot if 't wa'n't that 'ere cussed fisher come tu agin an' ketchin' holt of a saplin' wi' one of his fore paws!"

"Wal, I say fer 't," said Solon, "be they so terminatious o' life as that?"

"What for you ant tole him he dead, Sam? Dat all what was de matter wid it, he ant know when he dead!"

"Wal, I hed tu go tu work an' kill him agin, an' then I made aout tu git him hum 'thaout any more of his fluruppin' raound."

"I hain't never hed no chance o' studdyin' the nat'ral hist'ry on 'em," Solon observed, "but from what I've larnt 'oraclar, I jedge the name of fisher an' black cat don't no ways imply tu 'em. They don't ketch fish, an' consequentially they hain't fishers, an' though they be tol'able black, they don't resemblance the cat speshy no more 'n nothin' in the world. Hain't I right, Sammywell?"

"Sartinly you be," said Sam. "They don't never ketch fish—as I knows on—as mink an' auter does, but lives on squirrels an' mice an' birds an' rabbits, an' stealin' bait aouten saple traps; they're the beaters fer that. An' excep' fer their handiness in climbin' an' their hardness in dyin' the' hain't no cat abaout 'em. They're a overgrowed weasel or saple."

"They're putty scase nowerdays," Lisha said, "do' know 's they ever was plenty. Saple 's gittin' scase tew, but twenty, thirty year ago they was thicker 'n spatter. A man 'at onderstood it c'ld make his dollar a day easy trappin' on 'em. Ol' Uncle Steve Hamlin uster hev his lines o' saple traps sot fer milds through the woods every fall, clear'n tu the foot o' the Hump sometimes. Every little ways he'd hev a steel trap sot fer fisher that come along stealin' the bait aouten his deadfalls, an' he'd git consid'able many on 'em every year. But game 's a-gittin' scaser 'n' scaser. Samwill," he resumed, after some moments of meditative smoking, "if I luffted tu hunt an' fish as well as you du, I'd go daown tu the lake some fall 'long baout the fust o' September, tu Leetle Auter Crik, an' hunt ducks an' ketch pick'ril."

"I s'pose it's a turrible place for ducks," Sam said.

"Ducks!" cried Lisha; "good airth an' seas! I sh'ld think it was! Why, when I uster be daown that way a-whippin' the cat—an' I was a consid'arble sight ten year ago—they was thicker in the ma'shes—wild oats grows there, ye know—thicker in the fall 'n ever ye seen skeeters in a swamp in July. An' the 's Gret Auter an' Dead Crik jes' as full! The' 's a lawyer daown there name o' Pairpint uster go a-shootin' on 'em, with a feller tu paddle his boat, 'n' he'd git a heapin' bushil baskit full on 'em in a day ! 'N' they said 't he shot all on 'em a-flyin' ! Never shot none on 'em a-sittin' !"

"Like anough," Sam assented; "I've hearn tell o' folks 'at shot patridges a-flyin', but I never was bleeged tu. I c'ld allers git shots at 'em a-sittin'."

"An' pickril !" continued Lisha, "I never seen the beat on 'em. I uster go trollin' arter 'em wi' some on 'em, 'n' we'd hev each on us a big hook with a pork rind an' a piece o' red flannel on 't fer bait, an' a toll'able long line an' a short pole, 'n' we'd paddle 'long kinder easy on the aidge o' the channel, an' I tell ye we'd yarn 'em aout ! Ol' sollakers, tew; four, five, six paounds, an' one 't I seen weighed ten paound 'n' a half."

"By gol !" exclaimed Pelatiah, wide-eyed and wide-mouthed with wonder, "ten paoun' an' a half? He must ha' ben mos' 's big as one o' them 'ere whale fish 't they git lamp ile aouten on !"

"An' mushrats," said Lisha, continuing the relation of the wonders of the lowlands, "I've seen their haousen on the ma'shes in fall an' winter thick as ever ye seen hay cocks in a medder, 'most, an' hundreds of acres o' ma'sh with 'em sot jes' so thick. The' was Benham an' 'mongst 'em uster git as high as three hundred mushrat apiece, most every spring. These 'ere teamsters 'at hauls ore up here tu the forge says 'at ducks an' mushrat an' fish is jes' as thick there naow. That 'ould be the place fer ye, Samwill ! Ducks an' fish fer fun, an' mushrat fer profit."

"Probly dey bullpawt an' eel dah, ant it, Onc' Lasha? Ah wish Ah be dah too, me !"

"Eels! I guess the' is. Why, Ann Twine, you c'ld ketch as many o' the dum'd snakes in a night as you c'ld eat the nex' day, an' that 's a-puttin' on it high. Yes, an' the' 's pike an' bass, an' a gret fish 'at's got a bill like a shellduck, on'y longer, but they hain't good fer nothin'. An' the' 's sheepheads an' shad, 'n' more pa'ch an' punkinseeds 'n' you could shake a stick at in a fortnight, but nobody don't make no caount o' them, on'y boys fer the fun o' ketchin' on 'em. An' the' 's bowfins an' suckers 'n' I d'know what all. They hes gret times a-shootin' pickril airly in the spring, an' a-spearin' on 'em, tew."

"Wal, sah, Onc' Lasha, Ah can shoot it dat moosrat wid spear in winter w'en he'll live in haouse."

"Ketch mushrat with a spear! Oh, naow you go tu grass, Ann Twine. You'd ort tu hed a spear tu git them 'ere 'coons."

"You ant b'lieve it dat? You as' Injin if he ant git it moosrat dat way. Bah gosh! Yas! W'en ice all be frozed up, have it spear gat on'y but one laig baout so long as two foot, ver' sharp, wid toof on him an' woodle handlin' tree foot, four foot prob'ly long. Den walk slow, slow, ant mak it no nowse, to moosrat haouse. Den push him dat spear in quick! hard! raght in middly of it. You feel it spear shake, you gat dat moosrat, mebby one of it, two of it, sometam three of it, prob'ly. Den chawp in wid axe, tek it off, go nudder one jus' de same. Sometam git feefty, seexty all day."

"Wal, I do' know but what ye hain't a-lyin' fer onct, Ann Twine; it saounds kinder reas'nable. You want tu git ye thirty forty traps, Samwill, an' go daown there with Ann Twine an' his spear. Then ye'd hev a French cook an' live high duck, pea soup, an' roast mushrat three times a day."

"Bah gosh! Onc' Lasha, you ant steek you nose up dat moosrat! He pooty good for eat, Ah tole you!"

"Yes, yes; anybody 't eats snakes needn't spleen agin rats, sartin."

"Oh, Onc' Lasha," said the Canadian reproachfully, " eel don't snake, more as you was mud turkey."

"If I hed me a boat an' traps anough," Sam said, after some silent and thoughtful smoking, "I'd jes' like tu go daown there a-trappin' an' huntin' an' fishin'. An' then, arter I got a good shanty built, an' well tu goin', hev all on ye come daown a-visitin'."

"You jes' du it an' see 'f we don't, hey, boys?" And there was general assent. "Yes, Samwill, we'll tackle up a two-hoss waggin an' all go. We'll go tuckernuck, kerry aour own pervision; on'y mushrat an' fish we'll expeck you tu furnish, Samwill. Wal," Lisha continued, hoisting out his porringer of a watch and consulting it by the waning firelight, "it's a-gittin' late. Why, good airth an' seas! if 't ain't mos' nine o'clock! Peltier, 'f you've got that 'ere kittle licked aout, you c'n slick up a little raound, an' we'll go hum. No need o' bilin' tu-night, the' hain't sap 'nough in the store trough tu draound a chipmunk. Git the baskit an' Jurushy's bowl an' come along."

Then they filed out of the sugar camp on their homeward way, while far above them in the black growth of the mountain-side the hoot of an owl and the gasping bark of a fox voiced the solemnity and wildness of the ancient woods.

XVIII.

INDIANS IN DANVIS.

IT was fairly spring ; almost summer as the months go. Some patches and jagged lines of snow yet gleamed among the black growth on the northward steeps and in the gullies of the mountains, but the lower deciduous trees were in a green mist of young leaves, the woodside shade was dappled with the white moose-flowers, and the grass was green in the valley fields. The evenings had grown so short that to make anything of a visit before bedtime, Lisha's friends were obliged to come while daylight lasted. By that light, when the hylas were beginning to ring their shrill curfew, the old man was mitigating some customer's prospective torture by rasping the pegs on the inside of a boot, but to see the contortions of his face, turned aside as he bent over his hidden field of labor, one would think that he was inflicting self-torture, and that every scrape of the float was tearing the shoemaker's own tough hide. He made such a noise with his rasping that he first became aware of visitors when the forms of Joe Hill and Antoine darkened the open doorway. Then came Pelatiah and the Questioner, followed by Solon Briggs, and last of all Sam Lovel came across lots from Beaver Meadow Brook, bringing a dozen fine trout strung upon a birchen twig.

"Wal, Samwill, ben a-traoutin', hey?" said Lisha, emptying the scrapings out of the boot, and making an examination of the interior with his hand while he looked admiringly on the handsome fish. "Wal, they're neat ones, I swan! Ketched 'em in Beav' Medder Brook, did ye?" Yes, Sam caught them there. "Wal, they du say 't fishin' 's oncommon good this year; most everybody 't goes gits a good string on 'em. Oh, dear me suz! 'n' I hain't ben yit, nor tasted no fish but salt ones sen last summer."

"Bah gosh! Ah wish Ah ketch some bullpout or eel, bose of it, Ah don' care which, me," cried Antoine.

"Wal, Uncle Lisher, you sha'n't say that tu-morrer night," said Sam, seating himself on the cold stove and filling his pipe, "fer I'm goin' tu take these in tu Aunt Jerushy, an' you c'n hev your sheer on 'em fer breakfus'. Ben tu supper, I s'pose?"

"Why, Sam will, I'm a thaousan' times 'bleeged tu ye, but you'd orter keep half on 'em. You're a-robbin' yerself."

No, Sam was "cl'yed wi' traout, an' ketched these a puppus fer Aunt Jerushy 'n' you."

"Wal, thank ye a thaousan' times. Yes, I ben tu supper. I was makin' gardin tu-day, an' the smell o' the airth made me hungrier 'n a bear, so Jerushy got supper airly."

"Yes, Lisher," Solon remarked, "for a pusson of your sedimentary ockypations the' hain't nothin' more beneficient 'an a-gittin' aou'door;" and then, turning to Sam, "Did ye ever ketch traout with a fly, Sammywell?"

"No, I didn't never, but I hev wi' bumble-bees."

"Not a ra-al fly I don't mean," Solon explained. "That 'ere artist feller 't was raound here summer 'fore last—boarded tu Joel Bartlett's a spell, 'n' fixed up a paintin' shop in his barn—'stewed Joe,' he called it—he uster go traoutin' with a whipstock of a pole 'at took tu pieces, an' hed a little brass windlass onto it tu wind up his line, an' a mess o' feathers stuck on a hook for bait, 'at he called a arterfishual fly. He'd skitter it top of the water, an' onct in a while the' 'd be a traout fool 'nough tu grab it. Then he'd wind 'im up, an' then he'd let 'im scoot, 'n' then wind 'im up agin, an' so continner on till he got 'im all fattygued aout."

"Oh, yes, I seen 'im at it!" said Sam. "I went a-fishin' with 'im tew three times. 'N' he was toll'able lucky, tew; ketched half as many 's I did. He'd tost them little feather contraptions turrible handy when the brush wa'n't tew thick. I sh'ld like tu try it if I hed the rig. He hed a hull wallet full on 'em, all on 'em named, 'green ducks,' an' 'hatchels,' an' I d' know what all. It uster tickle me tu see him when he come tu a still pond hole, or a place where the brook tumbled over the rocks, or suthin' n'uther 't he liked the looks on. He'd lay daown his pole, an' back off, an' get fust one side o' the brook an' then t'other, or like 'nough on a stun right in the middle on 't, an' then aout with a lead-pencil an' a little blank 'caount book like, 'n' begin tu draw it off. He'd squint an' mark an' whistle an' mark a spell, 'n' then intu his pocket with book an' pencil an' go tu fishin' agin. A clever little creetur he was, an' took lots o' comfort bein' in the woods, an' a-fishin'. He tol' me 'at they ketched gret big salmon up Canady way wi' them feather flies."

"Bah gosh!" cried Antoine, pricking up his ears at the mention of his native province. "Yas, Ah'll see Anglish officy ketch dat so! Oh, big, big, big!"

"Oh, yes, sartinly," said Lisha, as he tied the straps of the completed boots together with a thong of leather, "I 'xpected you hed. Seen 'em ketched 't 'ould weigh a hunderd paound, hain't ye, Ann Twine?"

"Wal, sah, Onc' Lasha, not quat so big dat. Ah don' goin' tol' lie 'f you want it Ah do. De bigges' one Ah'll see ketch dat way he'll weigh jes' 'zackly nanty-nan paoun' an' fiftin ninches, dat's all."

"Hmph! A minny, wa'n't he?" said Lisha. "Wal, we're gittin' all of a color, white folks an' Canucks, 'n' I guess we'd better hev a light," whereupon he lit the candle, which sputtered for some minutes before it made itself visible in the twilight.

"Wal, folks," said Sam, breaking the silence that prevailed while the company watched the struggles of the feeble light, "the's suthin' in these woods 'at I never seen in 'em afore."

"Why, what on airth is it, Samwill?" Lisha asked.

"'Tain't a wolf, 'cause you seen one time o' the big hunt four year ago. 'Tain't a painter?"

"No, 'tain't a wolf nor a painter—I seen both—'n' 'tain't no four-legged critter—it's Injins!"

"Good airth an' seas, you don't say so!" cried Lisha; "hev ye got the' skelps in yer pockit, Samwill?"

"No," said Sam, laughing; "they've got 'em on their heads, an' hats a top on 'em, tew, for they hain't wild ones, but c'n talk English as well as Antwine here, but not ekal to Solon quite. Raal clever, candid sort o' fellers they be, an' c'nsid'able sosherble arter you git 'quainted with 'em."

"Haow many on 'em be they? A hull tribe on 'em? He ones an' she ones, an' poppooses on boards? Where be they, an' what they drivin' at?" So Lisha strung out his questions without waiting for an answer till he finished with the demand, "Tell us all baout 'em."

"Wal," said Sam, "tu begin 't the beginnin', I was fishin' Beav' Medder Brook 't other day an' come acrost a mockersin track in the sand, 'n' thinks says I to myself, Antwine's a-fishin' ahead on me, 'n' then thinks says I, he don't wear 'em sen he got tu be sech a Yankee; 'n' a little furder long I seen tracks o' tew wearin' mockersins, an' putty soon I smelt smoke, an' then come slap on tu tew dark-complected fellers settin' by a fire a-smokin' an' watchin' a woo'chuck roastin' on a stick stuck through endways an' int' the graound, an' behind of 'em was a gret roll o' suthin' 't I thought fust sight was luther, 'n' 't they'd ben a-stealin' from you, er less was goin' to give ye a job. Then I seen 't was birch bark. I says haow de du, 'n' so 'd they, but they didn't talk none till I soddaown an' loaded my pipe an' giv' 'em some terbarker. Then one on 'em says, 'Ketch um plenty fish,' lookin' at my string, an' 'twas a putty good un, 'n' I gin 'em a dozen tu piece aout their supper. Then they begin tu git toll'able sosherble, an' we hed quite a visit."

"Wal, I'll be dum'd! Samwill Lovel visitin' 'long with Injins!" cried Lisha, holding up his hands.

"Wal, he was," said Sam, "an' got c'nsid'able thick with 'em, 'n' I don't deny it. They said haow 't they 'd come clean up from Gret Auter Crik on tu Hawg's Back tu git bark 'at suited 'em tu make a canew, an' was goin' right back nex' day. I wanted turribly tu see 'em make a canew, 'n' tried tu coax 'em to du it here, 'n' I'd git some o' the teamsters tu kerry it daown tu Vergeens for 'em when they was goin'. But they thought their fam-

'lies 'at was camped daown there would be wonderin' if they stayed away so long. I tol' 'em 't we'd send word by the teamsters tu their folks, 'n' it come inter my head what you was tellin' 'baout huntin' an' trappin' daown there, 'n' 't this was a gret chance fer me tu git a boat made. So I dickered with 'em tu make me a canew, an' they talked an' talked together—I tell ye, their'n 's the language tu talk in the woods. It don't make no more noise 'n a little brook a-runnin', 'n' I don't b'lieve 't 'ould skeer a fox. Wal, fin'ly they 'greed tu, an' nex' day they went at my canew."

"Shaw!" said Lisha. "Why, Samwill, them Injin canews is tottlisher 'n a board sot up aidgeways! You can't du nothin' in one on 'em, only tip over. You hain't uster no kinder boat, say nothin' baout them aig-shell consarns. 'D ye ever see one? I hev, but never ondertook ridin' one on 'em."

"No, I never did, but I'm goin' tu in a few days. I guess I c'n navvygate it. I've crossed the Notch Pond stan'in' up on a saw lawg with my gun, more 'n onct, 'n' I guess a canew hain't much tottlisher 'n a rollin' lawg. Wal, I've hed a good time watchin' on 'em make it fer three days, 'n' I tell ye it's curous tu see 'em. Furst thing they made a frame the len'th an' shape the canew 's goin' tu be on top—jes tew strips of ash fastened together tu the ends, an' bars acrost, so"—illustrating his description with a diagram drawn on the floor with a bit of coal while all gathered about him. "Then they laid it daown on a level place they'd fixed an' drove stakes clus tu it agin the ends o' the cross-bars all raound, an' one tu each end o' the frame. Then they pulled up the stakes an' took the frame away, keepin' the stake-holes clear o' dirt very car'f'l, an' spread the bark daown on the place, an' then sot the frame back on jes' ezackly where it was afore, an' put some cedar strips on 't, an' big stuns top o' them. Then they slit the bark from the aidge up tu the frame every onct in a little ways, so, all raound, an' bent up the bark an' sot the stakes back in the holes, an' tied a bark cord acrost from top to top. Then they sewed up the slits, lappin' the bark over, ye see, an' sewin' it wi' black spruce ruts peeled an' split in tew, 'n' they're jest as tough as rawhide; luther-wood bark hain't no tougher. That's as fur as they've got yit, but nex' thing, 's nigh 's I c'n make aout, they cal'late tu raise the frame tu the top an' put some raves on aoutside and fasten 'em together an' then line the hull consarn wi' flat strips o' cedar drove in tight. 'N' then when they git the seams all daubed wi' spruce gum an' taller melted together it'll be all ready fer me tu—" "tip over," said Lisha, completing the sentence for him.

"Waal, now, I guess not," Sam drawled, "but baout the fust o' nex' week you c'n all come over tu the Forge Pond an' see."

"Wal, sah, Sam, Ah tol' you," said Antoine, "you wan' git good big lawg, an' Ah'll mek it you a canoe was good for sometings, me. Dat was damn sight gre' deal better for you as dat negg-shell Injin mek it."

Lisha snorted a contemptuous "Hmph ! 'T would be a putty-lookin' thing, Ann Twine. Guess 't 'ould look 's much like a stun boat's anything. But 't 'ould be comp'ny for ye, Samwill, fer I ha' no daoubt 't 'ould laugh and talk."

"Wal, sah, he look lak stun boat, he look goo' deal lak de boot you mek it, Onc' Lasha. Den prob'ly you call it ver' han'some, don't it?"

"Oh, shet up, you—" cried Lisha, shaking his hammer at the grinning Canadian. "I could make a gre't sight better boat aouten luther 'n you can aouten wood, I'll bate ye. I've hearn tell 't the Injins way aout West makes boats aouten luther, er bufflo hides anyway."

"Uncle Lisher," said Joe Hill suddenly, "is the' anything o' this story 't I hearn 'em talkin' over 't the store t'other day? Lemme see, was 't Wednesday or Thursday las' week, or was 't Friday? Yes, 'twas Friday, I know, 'cause M'ri sent by me fer a codfish, an' they hedn't got none, 'n' so we didn't hev' none fer dinner Sat'day, 'n' hed t' eat traout. Wal, they was tellin', some on 'em, haow 't you was a-talkin' o' sellin' aout 'n' goin' t' the 'Hio."

"Hey?" cried Lisha, giving a great start. "Oh, sho! Ye can't tell nothin' by what ye hear over tu that 'ere dum'd store. When they hain't talkin' baout hosses, 'n' when they be, they're a-lyin' an' gossipin' wus 'n a passel o' women tu a quiltin'."

"Onc' Lasha, if you goin' on 'Hio, Ah wan' you show me de way Ah'll fin' dat Conchety Pint you tol' me good whal 'go. Ah'll wan' go dar den."

"When yer time comes you'll go there, Ann Twine, 'thaout me showin', jest the same as spirits finds their way tu heaven an' t'other place. Say, Samwill, where d' ye keep yer Injin show? Der ye 'low anybody tu see it?"

"Oh, yes," said Sam, "you c'n see 'm fer nothin'; but I wouldn't go all tu onct, if I was you fellers. I kinder guess they don't like bein' gawped at no better 'n we du. They're camped daown on Beav' Medder Brook, a little ways 'bove the swamp. They're a-makin' a few baskits, an' bow-arrers fer boys, evenin's, an' most likely they'll be raound peddlin' on 'em 'fore long." Then, going over to light his pipe at the candle, he whispered, "I'll come over in the mornin', an' you 'n' I'll go an' see 'em, if you're a min' tu." Then aloud, "Wal, boys, I'm a goin' hum. Any on ye wanter ride 'long wi' me?"

Sam's invitation was at once accepted by all the visitors, who departed with him, each riding as he did, "shanks' horses;" and the shop was left in darkness again.

XIX.

THE BOY OUT WEST.

The prophet of the almanac had written along the June calendar, " Now, perhaps, a spell of weather," and his prognostication was being verified. For two days the rain had come down from the leaden sky, now in drenching showers, now in drizzles slanting to the earth before the gusty north-east wind, and still it came down. A robin in the apple-tree where his mate shingled their nest with her half-spread wings only left off "singing for rain" to preen his wet feathers, and then began again his broken song, cheerful enough but for its import to seem unsuited to its accompaniment, the splash of the rain, the doleful sighing of the wind, and the sullen roar of the swollen streams. The beaten-down blossoms that whitened the ground beneath the apple-trees, as if an unseasonable flurry of snow had fallen there, looked unlike blossoms now, but added another dreary feature to the dreary landscape ; the little brown house, without light or shadow on its walls ; the dripping, wind-swayed trees ; the sodden fields and woods ghostly behind the gray veil of rain, bounded by the blurred, flat wall of mountains, and roofed by the low sky.

When some of Lisha's friends, troubled by a vague rumor that had floated about the valley, visited the shop that day, they found it as cheerless inside as out, chilly, damp, and fireless, and unoccupied by its owner, whose apron lay upon the shoe-bench. Sam Lovel seated himself there, and when presently Lisha entered from the "house part," and he arose to give him his accustomed seat, the old man said, "Keep your settin', Samwill; I hain't workin' none tu-day," and after pottering in an aimless way among his stock and tools, set about lighting a fire. After repeated clearing of his throat, wherein the words seemed to stick, he said as he whittled the kindling, "Wal, boys, where ye goin' tu loaf evenin's next winter?"

"Why, right here, of course, Uncle Lisher," said Sam; "you hain't goin' tu turn us aout'door, be ye?"

"No, I hain't a-goin' tu turn you aou'door; I'm a goin' tu turn myself aou'door. The fact o' the business is, Jerushy 'n' I has baout made up aour minds tu go aout West an' live 'long wi' George."

"Wal, we heard some such talk," Sam said, "but we didn't scasely b'lieve the' was nothin' on it only talk, the' 's so much dum'd foolish gab a-goin' nowerdays. An'," he added, "I hain't heard none 'at saounded foolisher 'n this, tu me.'"

"Wal, naow, ye see," said Lisha, shutting the stove door, and after watching the fire a minute seating himself upon a sap tub, "me 'n' my ol' woman 's a-gettin' ol' 'n' ont' the daown hill-side, 'n' 't won't be many year 'fore we can't du nothin' scasely on'y set raound, 'n' we hain't got nob'dy tu ta' keer on us then on'y aour boy. He's sol' aout in the 'Hio, an' is goin' tu Westconstant tu live, a gret ways furder 'n the 'Hio, tew, three States beyund it, I b'lieve. 'Tain't a State yit, I guess Westconstant hain't, but on'y a terry-tory. Seems 'ough we couldn't stan' it tu hev him no furder off 'n what he is naow, an' so, ye see, we've c'ncluded tu go an' live 'long wi' him. He 's ben a-teasin' on us tu this ever so long, but I kinder hated tu, for I'm sorter growed in here, 'n' I hate tu naow, but I guess it's the best way."

"Wal, I guess 'tain't," said Sam, very decidedly. "You hev growed in, both on ye, an' it'll be julluk pullin' up tew ol' trees an' settin' on 'em aout agin, 'n' ye won't stan' it no better. No, Uncle Lisher, not a mite better 'n tew hemlocks took up an' sot aout. It'll be a diff'ent s'il o' land for ye, diff'ent breed o' neighbors—'f ye hev any—'n' they say 't that 'ere western country 's flatter 'n a pancake, 'thaout a maountin er a big hill tu be seen, so 's 't it tires a feller's eyesight clean aout a-trav'lin' so fur 'thaout nothin' tu stop it. An' no woods like aourn, they say. Haow long ye think ye can stan' it 'thaout the smell o' spruce in yer nose, er 'thaout seein' the ol' Hump er 'Tater Hill, er so much as little Hawg's Back er even Pig's Back a-stan'in' up agin the sky ?"

"Yas, sah, Onc' Lasha, dat so," Antoine put in. "You was be so lonesick you come dead raght off, bose of it, An' Jerrushy, too, you see 'f he ant !"

"An' if ye don't die," Sam continued, "the dum'd Injins 'll kill ye."

"Sho !" said Lisha, smiling grimly at Sam. "You're a putty feller, a-talkin' baout dum'd Injins arter bein' thicker 'n puddin' with 'em for a fortni't, 'n' they riggin' on ye aout wi' a canew 't you c'n navvygate 's a mushrat can his own body. Naow, r'aly, Samwill," he went on, hoping to change the subject, "when I seen ye gittin' into 't over there t' the Forge Pond, I didn't expect nothin' on'y tu see ye git a duckin', 'n' 'f I hedn't a knowed ye c'ld swim like a duck, I wouldn't ha' let ye git int' the dum'd crazy thing."

"Oh, wal," said Sam, impatiently, "my Injins is tame. I guess 't you'll find aout 't them painted, turkey-feathered cusses aout West is a diff'ent breed o' cats, with their war-whoopin' an' screechin', an' skelpin' ol' folks an' babies, 'n' the Lord knows what the devil's own work they hain't up tu."

"Sammywell's argyments is good," said Solon Briggs. "The' hain't nothin' more sartiner 'n that old, ann-cient indyviddywills hed ort tu continner tu remain in the natyve land 'at they was borned in."

"Good airth an' seas!" the old man roared, after listening with ill-concealed impatience, "what's the use o' yer talkin'? I tell ye I'm a-goin' 'f I don't live a week arter I git there! Hain't I tougher 'n a ellum gnurl? Hain't I fit your Injins' gran'thers tu Plattsburg? I c'n stan' the rackit, I guess! I c'n fight Injins agin, I guess! H'mph! ye talk 's if I was a ten-ye'r-ol' boy er a skeery little gal!" And then lowering his voice to a kindlier tone, "I hate tu go, 's I said afore. I allus luffted tu hev my neighbors raound me, 'n' 'I've hed good uns, an' got 'em yit, an' I hate dreffly tu leave 'em, 'n' hate tu leave the ol' place 'n' everything. But blood's thicker 'n water, 'n' I wanter see my boy, the on'y chick er child his mother 'n' I's got, 'n' eend my days wi' him. An' his mother y'arns arter him more 'n I du, an—wal, we're a-goin', an' the' ha' no tew ways baout it, ner no use a-talkin'. I've sol' aout tu Joel Bartlett, an' we've drawed writin's—an' that's the long an' short on't."

"Wal," said Sam, "if you're sot on it, 'n' everything 's all cut an' dried, the' *hain't* no use a-talkin'. But I sh'ld think 't you *might* ha' said suthin' tu some on us 'fore ye went so fur. 'T would ha' ben friendlier. I swear! I wish 't the dum'd torment 't invented that ere cussed Western country hedn't never ben borned! A-breakin' up fam'lies an' puttin' notions inter ol' folks's heads, blast him!" and said no more, but sat staring out at the gloomy landscape that, seen through the green and wrinkled panes of the long window, looked gloomier and more dismal than ever.

They spoke no more of Lisha's intended departure, and after a few feeble attempts at conversation, sat and smoked in silence till the day grew darker with the coming on of evening, and then the visitors departed.

XX.

BREAKING UP.

THOUGH Lisha's friends continued their visits to the shop, the rainy days and the evenings spent there were cheerless and gloomy ever after he declared his intention of deserting it. The forced conversation and feeble attempts to awaken the old convivial spirit were so much like those at a gathering about the bedside of one with the certain doom of death upon him, that Lisha said, one afternoon, when the sober guests had departed, "Wal, mother, I wish 't aour fun'al was over, an' we was in Westconstant. I'll be dum'd 'f I hain't 'baout sick o' bein' a live corpse! Good airth an' seas! When the boys comes up an' sets 'raound lookin' at me so solemn, I can een a'most feel the shoemake rhuts a-crawlin' raound my bones, 's if I was planted up yunder in the ol' graveyard. Oh, dear me suz! I wish 't George hed a' ben contented tu ha' stayed here! But seein' 't he wa'n't, the' don't seem 's 'ough the' was no other way only tu go. If little Jerushy 'd ha' lived, 'n' merried some likely feller, as in course she would, we might ha' stayed an' lived 'long wi' her. But it wa'n't tu be so. I do' know but I feel 'baout as bad a-goin' off an' leavin' her layin' up there so fur from us 's I du 'baout anything in the hull business. Poor little gal! She was a-goin' tu look julluk you."

"O father!" said Aunt Jerushy, with a blush mantling the wholesome old-age brown of her kindly face, as she intently scanned her purple-veined and wrinkled hands, "if she was ever tu, I do' know but it's best 'at she died when she was a baby."

"Wal, naow, Jerushy Chase, I shouldn't ha' wanted her tu looked no better 'n you did when you was a young womern, nor no better fer an' ol' womern. Folks hes got tu grow ol' 'f they live long 'nough, 'n' they can't keep all the looks no more'n they can all the feelin's o' young folks."

Uncle Lisha took a roundabout course on his way to the stove to relight his pipe, and stopped behind Aunt Jerusha's chair a moment to caress her gray head. The sensation must have been somewhat as if a mud turtle had crawled and slid over it, but it comforted her sad heart and brought a gleam of the light of youth into her old eyes. When he bent over and shyly kissed her cheek, the long disused endearment brought back old courting days so vividly that she cried, even as she returned it—"Why, Lisher Peggs! Hain't you 'shamed o' yerself?" and then glancing out of the window, "If there hain't Huldy Pur'n't'n! an' if she seen ye, haow she will be a-laughin' at us!"

"Good airth an' seas!" said Lisha, as in a shamefaced flurry he raked a handful of coals onto the hearth, "'f she hain't hed bussin' 'nough tu shet her maouth sen she an' Samwill made up, I miss my guess! They've made up lost time, I bate ye! Walk!" he shouted in response to Huldah's knock, and when she entered Aunt Jerusha's surprise was simulated so well that it would have done credit to a lady of fashion.

"An' so," said Huldah, after the mutual inquiries concerning the respective families had been made and answered, "you an' Uncle Lisher is r'ally goin' tu pull up stakes an' go t' the West? You do' know haow I hate 'tu hev ye. Seems 's 'ough the' wa'n't nob'dy only my own folks 'at seems so near tu me 's what you du!"

"Ta' keer, Huldy!" Lisha cried.

"Wal," said Huldah, blushing as red as the peonies in the posy bed by the doorstep, "I mean—wal," with a frank look and a happy little laugh, "I mean ol' folks near! The' hain't another place in Danvis where I c'n go an' hev a raal good sed daown, only jest here! An', Uncle Lisher, one little word 't you said that day 'at Sis was lost tol' me suthin' 't I didn't know afore, 'n' 't I was feared wa'n't so. 'N' naow you're a goin' tu the end o' the airth, 'n' I sha'n't see ye 'gin, maybe never!"

"Wal, naow, Huldy," said Aunt Jerusha, as she abstractedly rapped her snuff-box and looked nowhere, "like 'nough me an' Lisher won't be c'ntented in Westconstant, an' 'll wanter come back. An' 'f things tarve as I'm a-hopesin' they will, you an' Samwill 'll be settled daown, 'n' mebby you'd take us in."

"An' you'd be most welcome allers," said Huldah. "Seems 's 'ough," she said, as over and over again she gathered in her fingers and let go the hem of her checkered apron, "'at the' wa'n't nothin' much tu hender naow, sence Samwill faound Sis. Father, he was allers kinder set agin him 'cause he's allers a-huntin' an' shoolin' raound in the woods, but ever sence he hunted tu sech good purpose that day he hain't said not one word agin him. An' mother, she hain't never sot much noways. Seems 's 'ough the' wa'n't nothin' much tu hender naow." And as Huldah looked out of the east window of the kitchen, the hill-tops were glorified by the rays of the setting sun, all the rugged steeps were shining, and the shadowy ravines were hidden from her gaze; and so the way of life shone before her, smooth and unshadowed in the light of love.

When Gran'ther Hill had berated Lisha and Jerusha to all his heart's content, so obtainable to Joseph and his wife and the hushed bevy of children, as "a pair o' ol' idjits a-goin' off beyund the reach o' all God's massies tu the' own fun'al," he marched down upon them one pleasant day to the tune of "'The Road to Boston,'" dolorous enough for a dead march as whistled through his thin lips, with no supporting ranks of teeth behind them. When he was established in the arm-chair that Jerusha set for him after beating the cushion into inviting softness, he cast a severe and frowning look upon the couple, and demanded, marking each word with a thump of his cane upon the floor, " Wal, Lisher, hain't you 'shamed o' yerself, a-desartin' of yer country at your time o' life? I never 'd ha' thought it of a man 'at hed fout tu Plattsburg battle. But that was in York State. You wouldn't ketch a man 'at hed fout tu Hubbar'to'n an' Bennin'to'n leavin' Varmaount, 'at he 'd fout for! No, sir! Shet yer head, I tell ye!" as Lisha attempted a word in his own defence. " Ye needn't tell me nothin' 'baout George! He might come back here 'f he wanted tu live wi' ye so bad! Varmaount's good 'nough place for anyb'dy tu live in—a dum'd sight tew good for some folks, as me 'n' Ethin, 'n' Seth, 'n' Remember, 'n' 'mongst us showed some o' them 'ere lan' jobbers! Dum yer 'Hios an' Westconstants! West damnations they be, the hull on 'em, full o' fever 'n' aag an' snakes an' Injins an' all God's cusses ! Ye'd better stay an' die where ye growed ! I hope ye won't die in a month arter ye git there, but ye will, both on ye ; see 'f ye don't ! 'F ye don't shake the skin off'n yer bones with the agur, the snakes 'll bite ye, 'n' 'f the snakes don't bite ye, the Injins 'll skelp ye !"

"Good airth an' seas !" cried Lisha, rubbing his bald pate, "a 'tarnal sight o' satisfaction they'd git a-skelpin' me. But the' hain't no Injins tu hurt there, I tell ye !"

"Wal, the' 's 'nough. The' 's snakes 'n' fever 'n' aag ; they'll fix yer flint, 'f ye don't git draownded in that 'ere canawl, an' a turrible disagreeable, nasty place it is tu git draownded in, I s'pose. I do' wanter hear ye talk ! Ye can't tell me nothin' 'baout it ! I done my duty, an' gin ye fair warnin'," and the old Revolutioner stamped off without listening to a word from them.

"Wal, I say for 't," said Aunt Jerusha, looking after him, " 'f he don't een a' most make a body skeered o' goin' !"

"Humph !" Lisha snorted, contemptuously, " he do' know nothin' 'baout it. He do' know beans 'baout anything 'at is er happened sen' the ol' war."

One day Joel Bartlett came in, and after solemn deliberation and a more than ordinary puckering of his mouth, said, "Friends, Jemimy an' me hes hed some weighty consideration consarnin' your givin' up here an' goin' away. Thee knows, Lisher, at thy little place fits in very handy 'long o' mine—in fact, it is part o' the original pitch of ol' Hezekier Varney's tew-hunderd acre lot, an' is quite desirable. But I hev' felt it bore in upon me tu come an' tell you, thee an' Jerushy, that if you feel misgivin's as tu the wisdom o' breakin' up here an' goin' West tu your son, I am willin' tu give thee back thy deed, which it hain't been sot in the records, an' I am willin'—yes, I am willin'," after a little inward struggle, "tu du so withaout no consideration—only thee shall pay for the drawin' o' the writin's, which is diffunt from what we agreed."

"No, Joel," Lisha answered, "I'm 'bleeged tu ye, but aour minds was made up tu start on, an' I hain't a-goin' tu play baby naow. We're goin'."

"Wal," Joel said, with a sigh of relief, "I felt as 'ough it was my duty tu make thee this offer, an' naow I feel clear. Whatever comes, your Heavenly Father 'll be as nigh tu ye in the perraries as he hes ben in the shadder o' the maountains," and he went home feeling that he had done all that his conscience demanded for its ease.

By and by came the sad and painful breaking up and the auction sale of their non-portable goods, such household gods as the old clock that had marked, with its slow beats, the uneventful and comfortable course of more than half their life; the big wheel and the little wheel that had both hummed many tunes to Aunt Jerusha's touch, and were dear to her. And so to her was the churn, but Uncle Lisha saw it go to a low bidder with a feeling of relief in final separation, and a thrill of revengeful pleasure as he thought of the unhappy hours spent in pounding stubborn churnings encased in its red-painted staves. It mitigated the pangs of parting with them to know that Sam Lovel had bought the clock (with an inward resolve that it should some time resume its old place in the kitchen corner), and that the spinning-wheels had gone to the Puringtons. The big wheel, Mrs. Purington said, "'ould be handy for Huldy when she went tu haousekeepin', though the flax wheel wa'n't much 'caount, sen' everyb'dy 'd gin up raisin' flax." Solon Briggs suggested that it would be "a val'able relickt of ancient past times tu Huldy's future pregenitors." Sam also bought the shoe-bench, saying that it was a " mighty comfortable seat tu set in an' smoke, with a handy place for a feller's terbacker, as well as bein' a good place tu clean a gun." He was strongly tempted to buy the favorite cow, so gentle that even Huldah might milk her, though she never should, but with the fear of his stepmother before him, he let the cow go to Joseph Hill.

"Dat damn hol' long John Dark!" said Antoine, when the giant of the turkey shoot bid off the old horse after the Canadian had gone beyond the limit of his resources in bidding. "'F he ant be for he, Ah'll have it some hawse for swaup! Den Ah'll go Vairgenn, an' prob'ly get tree, prob'ly fave dollar for boot! What dat John Dark wan' come 'way ov' here for spile 'em up my buy dat hawse, hein!"

"Why, Ann Twine," said Lisha, "I'd ha' knocked ol' Bob in the head 'fore I'd ha' let 'im go tu a Canuck tu 'buse an' starve!"

"Bah gosh! you call it bruse heem for swaup it for hawse better as he'll was?"

John Dart made his way to Aunt Jerusha and said: "Mis' Peggs, I'll take good keer o' the ol' hoss, an' won't never drive 'im fast—'thaout 't is keepin' up wi' the percession tu fun'als, which I'm hopesin' won't come often, 'n' I won't never sell 'im, ner give 'im tu nob'dy only God A'mighty—I'll du that when he gits so 's 't he can't enj'y airthly life."

"Thank ye kindly, Mister ——?"

"John Dart is my name, marm," said the giant, bowing almost to the level of her sun bonnet.

"Thank ye kindly, Mister Dart, an' I'm dreffle glad 'at Bob hes fell intu sech good hands. He's ben a faithf'l creetur tu us, an' it's worried me dreffly thinkin' o' what might be become on him."

The "vandew" was over at last, and the old couple's hold on their old life was loosened with sore wrenchings of their heartstrings. Now that their hearthstone was cold and the little brown house was home no longer, they tarried with Joseph Hill during the short time of awaiting the day of departure. Lisha wandered about aimlessly, uncomfortable in idleness and continual wearing of his best clothes, taking long looks at old familiar scenes that he felt he was soon to leave forever. He went with Aunt Jerusha to the little hillside burying-ground, which had grown surprisingly populous with dead since they attended the first burial there, awed then in the strange presence of death, who had now become so frequent and familiar a visitor that his coming was but briefly noted. There under the widespread canopy of the sumachs and among the rank growth of golden-rod they bade a silent farewell to the sunken graves of fathers and mothers, and the short green mound that so many years ago had hidden from their sight their baby daughter—always and forever a baby daughter to them.

"An' naow, mother," said Lisha, making frequent use of his "bendinah" as they turned away from the quiet place of everlasting rest, "we've said good-by tu them 'at's nighest tu us. Aour rhuts is putty nigh pulled up."

XXI.

THE DEPARTURE.

Toward the end of summer Lisha and his wife were ready to begin their journey. The day of departure had come, and many of their old neighbors had gathered at Joseph Hill's to bid them farewell. Among these were Joel Bartlett and his wife ; he with solemn words of advice and consolation, she full of kind thoughtfulness for the comfort of their departing friends, who, though "world's people," were endeared to her through life-long neighborhood. "I trust, Lisher," said Joel, after puckering his lips so tightly that the boys who had come to behold the exodus thought the event was to be celebrated by the long-deferred whistle, "'at thee is clear in thy mind 'at thee is a-walkin' in the way 'at is lit by the in'ard light, an' I hope the path'll be made smooth an' pleasant tu thy feet, an' them o' thy companion, an'—" "'F he wore hees own boot?" Antoine asked, in an undertone. And Gran'ther Hill broke in from his seat in the doorway, shaking his cane at the shoemaker—"Wal, it won't, Lisher ! You 'll find it a hard rhud fer tu travil, I tell ye ! A hard rhud fer tu travil, wi' fever 'n' aag, an' snakes, an' Injins ! An' the canawl, an' all ! When ye git a chance tu pint yer gun 't an Injin, pint a leetle 'fore he does, and shoot tu kill !" And he came down and shook hands with Lisha and his wife.

Tom Hamlin lurked shyly about the outer edge of the circle, and the man who always asked questions was present, silent, but his face and figure a standing interrogation point.

Huldah's pretty face was hidden in Aunt Jerusha's sunbonnet, and reappeared with tear-stained cheeks, while her mother wiped away her own sympathetic tears with alternate corners of her apron, and her father coughed loudly to cover the break in his voice. And so came farewell to old friends and old scenes.

After the kindly fashion of those days, some of their neighbors accompanied them to the place where they were to embark in the canal-boat that would take them the length of "Clinton's big ditch" on their way. Pelatiah drove the lumber wagon whereon was piled the "housel stuff" reserved from the "vandew." Then came a like conveyance, driven by Sam Lovell, and carrying Lisha and Jerusha, Joe Hill and his wife, Solon Briggs and Antoine, and a day's provisions for the party. They jolted over the rough road and through the little hamlet that the forge and store and tavern gave life to, and then taking the road along the bank of the noisy little river, the old people turned their backs upon the green wall of the mountains and entered on their long journey westward. Lisha was as cheerful as could be expected when his heart was heavy with the sorrow of leaving his old home, and he was suffering the discomfort of his high-collared, tight-sleeved best coat and the weight of his bell-crowned hat. He pointed out the farm where the first settler of Danvis had "pitched," the hill where Pelatiah's grandfather killed a panther, discoursed of the changes that had come since he first knew the town, made some strained efforts at joking with Antoine, and talked on and on when he had nothing to say. Aunt Jerusha wept silently in the seclusion of her new gingham sunbonnet, comforting herself with frequent pinches of snuff that afforded her an excuse for as frequent use of her handkerchief.

At noon they stopped to bait their teams and eat their lunch under some wayside trees and then went on. In the middle of the afternoon they entered the little city that marked the end of the first stage of the old people's journey, and the wonders of its few three-story buildings, its three churches, and the court-house perched upon the crest of a ledge, in which, Lisha told them, "the leegislatur sot onct," so dazed Pelatiah that he nearly missed finding the way to the wharf where the canal packet lay. There new wonders met his astonished gaze. A rifle shot up stream, the river almost as wide as the length of the forge pond, the largest sheet of water he had ever seen till now, foamed and thundered down a precipice forty feet high, and then its vexed waters writhed along a deep, broad reach, past the wharves, where lay the canal-boats and the little steamer that was to tow them to the lake and then to Whitehall.

Lounging about these strange immense craft were the surly or saucy canal-boatmen, upon whom the young mountaineer looked with awe, for they were travelled men who must have seen nearly all of the great world, having been more than once to the end of the canal and back again, and some, it was said, had even beheld the wonders and glories of that almost fabulous city by the sea, New York.

"In an airly day," said Lisha, "some o' the Yorkers

built 'em a gris' mill on them falls, an' Ethan Allen an' his Green Maountin Boys come an' drove 'em off an' hove the millstuns over the falls, or some says inter a big pothole nigh the top, 'n' 't they're a layin' in the bottom on't naow. Right along here where these 'ere wharfs an' stores be, McDonner's ships was built time o' the last war; ships a gre' d'l bigger 'n them canawl boats be, Peltier. I worked here a-haulin' timber to build 'em on, an' 'twas hurryin' times, I tell ye, with the British threatenin' the hull time. We hauled a big stick here aouten the woods, for a keel, it was, wi' three yoke o' oxen, an' at it the ship carpenters went full chisel, an' in six weeks I b'lieve, it wa'n't no more, from the day 't was cud daown, the ship was all ready to go int' the water! That's the way they did things in them times. A spell arter that the British come in their gunboats to destr'y the 'Merican vessels here, but they didn't git no furder 'n the maouth o' the crick, for aour folks hed a little fort there, a leftenant name o' Cassin' commandin' on't, an' they drove the British boats off. They call it Fort Cassin' yit, but 't ain't nothin' but some banks o' airth, an' wa'n't then. When aour ships got all ready they went off int' the lake, an' bimeby come Plattsburg fight. We all rallied aout, an' th' was lots o' Green Maountin Boys tu it, me 'mongst the rest on 'em, skeered 'nough, but no notion o' runnin'. We fit an' fit on land, an' the ships fit on the water, till arter a good spell aour ships licked their'n, an' then the British we was fightin' run, an' I tell ye the backs o' their 'tarnal red cuts was a dum sight the best lookin' side on 'em 't we'd seen yit. That's all the folks-fightin' 't ever I done, or ever wan' tu. That 'ere big stun buildin' over yunder where the flag 's a-flyin' is the gov'ment a'snal. The's muskits an' cannon 'nough in it tu rig aout a hull army. 'N' there! that pussy ol' red-nosed feller comin' a hossback 'long the road 's the major 't bosses it. Nothin' tu du but draw his pay, fo' five hundred dollars a year, I s'pose, an' drink ol' Jamaky sperits an' sweet wine, an' loaf 'raound.''

With such discourse Lisha entertained his friends till nightfall, when he and Jerusha went to their berths in the packet and they to their inn, excepting Antoine, who having dug some worms, and borrowed a pole and line of a compatriot, went fishing for bullpouts.

Next morning came the sorrowful leave-taking, and after much bustle and shouting and swearing by the captains and crews of the steamboat and canal boats, wherein the bold mariners of the canal having had the practice and experience of greater and more frequent opportunities, greatly outdid their rivals, the little flotilla got under weigh. The fussy little steamer coughed and churned its way down the beautiful river, and as it dragged the packet out of sight behind a wooded bend, the sturdy figure of the old shoemaker was seen standing in the stern beside the bowed form of his wife waving a last farewell with his red "bendina."

"There they go," said Sam Lovel, turning sadly away. "There they go, julluk tew ol' trees tore up by the ruts an' driftin' daown stream."

XXII.

THE WILD BEES' SWARM.

ONE day, a little more than a year later, when the blue September sky arched the valley, and the afternoon sun shone warm into it, and the bees were busy among the asters and golden-rods in the little graveyard that overlooked Uncle Lisha's old homestead, Sam Lovel came pushing his way slowly through the thicket of sumachs. Under his arm he carried his bee-box, which, after looking about him a moment, he set upon the top of a little gravestone. When he had watched for a minute through the glazed lid the two or three little prisoners his box held, he carefully removed the cover and backed a few paces away. His eye caught the moss-grown inscription on the stone—" Jerusha, daughter of E. and J. Peggs ; departed this life"—he had to bend down the heads of everlasting to read the remainder—" Sept. the 10, 18—"

He reaped away the everlastings with his knife and cleaned the moss from the letters before he took time to notice that one of his bees had climbed to the edge of the box and taken wing, circling a few feet above it, and then sailed straight toward the house ; and then another and another arose and went off in the same course.

" Wal, naow, that's cur'ous, hain't it, Drive ?" said Sam, addressing his dog, who was making himself comfortable on the grass near him, and now answered his master with a lazy beat of his tail. Sam had hardly got his pipe alight and begun to take his ease beside the dog, when back came the bees with some companions and settled into the box.

"All right," said Sam. "Le's move up," and going cautiously to it, he shut the lid, tapped the side till the bees arose from the comb in the bottom, when he shut the lower slide, took up the box and moved on in the direction the bees had taken to within a few rods of the house. Then he opened the slide and then the cover, and when the bees had filled themselves again, they sailed away with their freight as before. They soon returned and were again imprisoned till Sam had set the box on one of the posts of the garden-fence. Again he gave them their liberty, and in ten minutes a hundred bees were buzzing to and fro between the box and a knot-hole high up in the gable of the shop.

"Yes, sir," said Sam, laughing softly, "the's a swarm under the cla'b'rds o' the shop, jes' as sure 's your name 's Drive! Wal, they c'n stay there for all o' me."

He went around to the front of the house, stepping carefully lest he should tread on Aunt Jerusha's posies, uncared for now and running wild: China-asters, sweet-williams, and pansies struggling in a matted tangle of May-weed, posy beans and morning-glories wandering away from the posts of the stoop to climb the tall pig-weeds. Two squirrels stopped chasing each other over the roof and along the rattling clapboards to scoff at the intruder, and a woodchuck sounded his querulous whistle and scuttled under the shop as Sam approached it. The door was half open, and he almost expected to hear the hearty hail of his old friend; but a chance-sown poppy growing in a crack of the sill, and the fallen petals of its last flower withering undisturbed on the worn threshold, told mutely how long it had been untrodden by the foot of man. When Sam looked into the empty shop, where nothing was left to tell of its former use but a faint waft of the old familiar odor, the sconce and its mouse-nibbled candle-end, a broken last and a rubbishy heap of leather scraps, a partridge sprang from the floor and, hurtling through the open window, went sailing away to the woods.

"The fog o' the ol' stories hangs 'raound here yet," Sam soliloquized, "an' wild creeturs takes as nat'ral as tu the woods tu Uncle Lisher's shop. Come, dawg."

www.ingramcontent.com/pod-product-compliance
Lightning Source LLC
Chambersburg PA
CBHW031441160426
43195CB00010BB/809